Fisherman's Fall

RODERICK HAIG-BROWN

Fisherman's Fall

Nick Lyons Books

Printed in the United States of America

10 9 8 7 6 5 4 3 2 1

Library of Congress Cataloging-in-Publication Data

Haig-Brown, Roderick Langmere, 1908-1976.
Fisherman's fall / Roderick Haig-Brown.
p. cm.
Reprint. Previously published: New York : Crown, c1975.
ISBN 0-941130-55-X : $11.95
1. Fishing—Northwest, Pacific. 2. Pacific salmon fishing—Northwest, Pacific. 3. Steelhead fishing—Northwest, Pacific.
I. Title.
SH464.N6H35   1987
799.1'755—dc19   87–17626
CIP

Contents

V. AQUARIUM NOTES

VI. CONCLUSIONS

Preface to the 1975 Edition

Fall is the time that most of the migratory runs come back to the rivers here on the Pacific Coast of North America. All our five species of Pacific salmon come home then except for a few early-running chinooks and cohos. Most of the winter-spawning cutthroat trout run into their rivers then. The last of the summer-run steelhead and the first of the winter runs almost close the gap between themselves. It is the liveliest, most exciting time of all the year. Gulls and eagles, goldeneyes and mergansers, bears and mink and raccoons all come down to the rivers.

We know so much more about these migratory runs than we once did: where they go in the oceans, how they move through the ocean years, even a little of how they find their way back to their rivers of origin. We know something of their freshwater needs and timing. We know that each species of fish that runs to a major watershed has many subraces that are peculiarly adapted, each to its own particular part of the watershed. We know that these wild stocks have wide genetic variations that can enable them to survive and rebuild in the face of disease or natural disaster. We know much more than this—about survival rates and growth rates, the timing of downstream migration, the importance of feeding in the estuaries, and the river's plume of freshwater flow over salt. We know we can tamper with these things only at great risk to the survival of the runs.

How much more is there that we don't know and should have learned by now? In British Columbia we do not yet recognize fish production as one of the uses of fresh water, yet without fresh water we would have neither salmon nor trout nor char nor eulachons, and we should be much the poorer for that. We know that logging and most other forms of land use can be very damaging to watersheds unless carefully controlled, but we have not yet learned how to exercise this control. We know that hatcheries are of doubtful value at best, and ruinous at worst, and we know there are better and more productive alternatives. Yet we haven't examined those alternatives thoroughly and we haven't learned ways of putting them to work. We know that streams can be protected and their productivity substantially increased, but we haven't as yet really learned how to go about it or cared to put real effort into the learning. We still trust engineers and technologists, or say we do, which might be all right if the fish responded to them with equal faith, but they don't. The fish respond to their own biology and to the fresh- and saltwater conditions that serve it.

We know so much and so little about the anadromous salmons and trouts. What we do know would be enough to save them if we put it to full use. In British Columbia, where we are not cursed with main stem dams on our major rivers, we could hope to return all our streams to full fertility and maximum production. It is a dream I like to dwell on when I am along the fall rivers. The salmon themselves clean and refresh the gravels of the stream bottom in their spawning activities; later their dead bodies feed fertility to the stream itself, benefiting all the creatures that use it, including their own progeny. There is a charm of interdependency in all this, some magic statement of unity and completeness that gives promise of a return to rivers of primitive abundance. It is more than a dream really. I believe we can achieve it, though there may have to be a little more order and regularity in the new abundance.

Roderick Haig-Brown
Campbell River, B.C.
April 1975

PART ONE

The Scene

1. *Fall Defined*

FALL COMES QUITE GRADUALLY ON THE Pacific Coast of Canada, so gradually that one scarcely knows when or whether it has arrived. Sometimes a storm blows up from the south early in August, with a cold, wet rain that brings a subtle change. Yet it is certain the sun and the hot days will come again and perhaps hold on through most of September. If they do, there will be early frosts to turn the leaves and insist that fall is here. More often a storm around Labor Day brings the change. Again, the dry hot days may return after it, perhaps bringing woods' closure and forest fires; but the change will be clear; fogs will force in from the ocean and the morning dew will be everywhere. With or without frost, the leaves will turn and begin to fall.

Fall is also in the return of the salmon to their rivers—not, of course, in the early king salmon runs that come to a few rivers in May or the early running races of sockeye, but in the typical pink salmon runs that come in towards the end of July. With their coming the great fall movement to the coastal rivers begins. The big kings follow quickly, in August and September. A few cutthroat trout may have begun their movement even a little before the humpbacks. The cohos come in with the rains of September and October, the chum salmon are close behind them, and often with them, in October and November. Well before the last of the salmon is dead, it is December and unquestionably winter.

Fall fishing is a revival after the quieter times of summer. Cooler nights and the melt of early snowfall in the mountains bring falling water temperatures and rains freshen the streams. Shadows are longer, shielding the pools. The fish are more active and there is a touch of urgency about it all, a feeling that it cannot last very long so one had better get out and be doing. After all, there have been falls when the heavy rains came early and suddenly, the streams flooded and everything was over before it had started. Occasionally such memories trick me into going out and searching for runs before they have come in, using up fishing time that might have been better spent a week or two later. But I am not at all sure this is ever a matter for real regret, because there is always something around in the fall and one can come upon surprises—a few migrant fish running ahead of their time, an unexpected hatch that brings resident fish on the feed or even some phase of movement wholly unsuspected in other years. Few movements of wild creatures run to an exact timetable, year in, year out, and few are without their aberrant individuals; and few of us know our own familiar waters quite so well as we think we do.

Fall is almost everywhere a prime fishing time. In early fall the arctic grayling reaches his peak of fatness and condition and the lake trout move towards shallower water and their spawning. Brown trout and eastern brook trout are fall spawners, the cutthroat is chiefly a winter spawner; all three take on a special beauty of coloration as maturity approaches, echoing the reds and golds of the falling leaves. One may look for the bright and silvery immature fish among these and even prefer him, but his beauty is less vivid and he is not set apart as a sign of the season.

There is much pleasure in fall fishing, especially on streams where salmon run. But one does not have to fish to make the most of it. Of all times of the year on the Pacific watershed, fall is the most exciting. Spring is the most beautiful time, summer perhaps the most delightful, winter the most testing, at least physically; but fall is the time of movement. Anyone who passes along the streams may see it and feel it. Even when I am hunting ruffed grouse or Wilson's snipe, I find myself pushing out to the stream edges, following them where I can, looking down into the fall-dark water to search for the salmon's movements among the drifting leaves. Traveling fish roll up in the heavy water, spawners splash and work and struggle on the shallows, exhausted fish shelter in the eddies. Bear trails are worn and muddy along the banks, prints of coon and mink show up on sand bars and other soft places. Mallards, mergansers and goldeneyes start up from the quieter reaches where they have been feeding on salmon already dead. Being a fisherman, one looks for trout among the salmon or checks the brightness of the cohos to see if any are still worth taking, one studies the pools and runs and, when they are unfamiliar, promises oneself to come

back some other time to test them. But none of this is
necessary. It is enough to be on hand at this solemn, untidy
time when the woods are wet and quiet and the salmon are
completing their cycle.

To some people, the thought that the salmon, all Pacific
salmon of all species, die very soon after spawning is a
depressing one. They see in it only decay and waste, a sort
of pathetic frustration of life. This is a natural view, but it
does not question deeply enough; the end of the salmon is
not death and corruption, but only fall, the autumn of their
cycle. They come to the spawning gravels in all their brilliant colors—reds, browns, greens, gray and black and
golden. Like the autumn leaves above them, they have their
time of fierce glory. Then the frosts and the rains and the
winds come. The leaves become torn and sodden and dulled
and in their time they fall, covering the ground, drifting
with the stream currents, piling against the rocks and shallows. But within the trees life is still strong and self-
renewing.

As the winds stir and drift the dying leaves, so the waters
drift and stir the dying salmon against the gray-brown
gravels of the stream beds. But under those gravels life is
strong and secret and protected in the buried eggs, the real
life of the race. Fungus grows on the emptied bodies, as it
grows among the fallen leaves; they collect in the eddies
and strand on the gravel bars and the bacteria of change
work in them to make a new fertility. In spring life will
burst from the gravel as it bursts again from the trees, into
the massive yield of the new cycle. Death is seldom more
fleeting or more fertile than this.

The salmon runs are not the whole story of fall on the

Pacific Coast streams, but no one can fish there and not be aware of them and no fisherman can fail to be curious about them and concerned for them. A great commercial fishery depends on them. Tens of thousands of anglers go out each year to catch them in the salt water and every angler who fishes a migratory stream sees them and finds his sport, directly or indirectly, through them, for the power of the runs persists through the year and affects all other fish.

But the salmon runs are more than this. They are a last true sample of the immense natural abundances of the North American continent. They have been damaged and reduced in many places, it is true, and in some places, especially the Columbia River, the damage is great and permanent. But they remain a massive abundance, complex and wonderful, throughout most of their range, and throughout much of it their potential of natural abundance is as great as ever, while new understanding of their ways and needs suggests that increase over the natural abundance may well be possible through man-made assistance.

I feel this as a special challenge to mankind in general and to North Americans in particular. Is there one wild thing on the face of the earth that we can use and live with in reasonable harmony, preserving and even enhancing its natural magnificence? The record to date suggests there is not, that our own demanding and untidy living habits must always destroy, if not the creature itself, then certainly the living space it depends upon. Yet for the salmon it would seem there is some hope. It is a valuable creature, fundamentally and irreplaceably valuable as a source of food in a hungry world. Much of its living space is the sea, an area of the globe that we have not so far found it possible or necessary to change or damage very greatly. The rest is in the streams, which our own interests demand that we keep as clean and pure as possible. Unhappily, we often consider it convenient to obstruct, divert or otherwise abuse them, but there is at least a possibility that we may develop beyond these primitive practices in time to save a good deal for the salmon.

This, I admit, is a rather special viewpoint in an age of relentless change and destruction. It reflects intangible values and instinctive, even primitive, sympathies that are not much in favor today. But when I come to write of a fisherman's autumn I am bound to think first of the salmon and then, remembering the sense of wonder they have stirred in me through nearly forty seasons, I am bound to plead their case and tell what little I know of them. I hope they will long be here, in the waters of California, Oregon, Washington, British Columbia and Alaska, to stir fresh wonder in the hearts and minds of later human generations.

PART TWO

Pacific Salmon

1. *Origins*

ONE OF THE FIRST QUESTIONS ASKED about Pacific salmon is: "Are they true salmon?" The answer is that they are, but that the matter will stand a good deal of examination and is well worth examination.

Many creatures of the new world have common names that have been transferred from the old world—the American robin, for instance, is properly a thrush, not even nearly related to the little European robin; the lovely American "sparrow hawk" is closely related to the kestrel, not the European sparrow hawk; the American "partridge" is a ruffed grouse; the eastern brook trout is a char rather than a trout; the "blackfish" of the Pacific Coast is not a blackfish at all, but a killer whale. The examples could be multiplied endlessly. Occasionally they are confusing, more often they are not; usually they reflect the homesick settler's search for the familiar, but often, too, they reflect the keenness of his observation.

The Atlantic salmon of the east coast was no problem at all to the early settlers. He looked like a salmon, behaved like a salmon and was in fact exactly the same fish they had known as a salmon in Europe—*Salmo salar*, the fish the Romans had called "the leaper."

The early explorers and settlers of the Pacific slope had no difficulty in recognizing the fish they found there as salmon, but there were differences. First of all, there was the almost incredible abundance; then there were the different sizes and species, running at different times, and the distortions of shape and color that came with sexual maturity. Salmon, yes, clearly salmon of a sort, but not *true* salmon, not the real thing. Their very abundance counted against them. How could anything so common, so prolific, be a king among fishes?

Inevitably there was much argument about it, learned and otherwise. The final consensus was, and is, that the Pacific fish is a salmon, but of a different genus. The formal classification accepted today is as follows: suborder, Salmonoidea; family, Salmonidae; genus, *Oncorhynchus*, of which there are six species and perhaps several subspecies. The Atlantic salmon belongs in the same family, but is grouped with the trouts, both Atlantic and Pacific, in the genus *Salmo*. Even so, the physical differences that establish this generic rating are rather small. In *Salmo* the bones are generally heavier and the anal fin is shorter, having twelve rays or less while *Oncorhynchus* has thirteen or more. There are small differences in skull structure and in the development of the teeth. But the most impressive biological difference is in the fact that all Pacific salmon, without exception, die shortly after spawning, while the Atlantic salmon and the trouts, including the steelhead, may live to spawn several times.

The obvious conclusion is that the Atlantic and Pacific salmons have a common ancestor not too far back in geological time. Beyond this all is necessarily speculation, but a recent and closely reasoned paper by Dr. Ferris Neave* gives strong direction to the speculation and I for one am happy to accept its conclusions.

Dr. Neave goes back to a time between one and two million years ago when the Atlantic and Pacific were connected across the arctic in such a way that cold-temperate fishes and other life could pass back and forth with some ease. At this time the Atlantic salmon or its direct progenitor probably populated many of the North Pacific streams on both the American and the Asiatic side. About a million years ago the arctic passage was blocked and the Atlantic and Pacific salmonoid populations became isolated. In the course of this isolation the Pacific stock gradually adopted the habits and characteristics of the steelhead trout, a fish whose close relationship to the Atlantic salmon is apparent to any angler who is reasonably familiar with both species.

Today the steelhead or its landlocked form, the rainbow trout, is present in all waters tributary to the great semicircle of the North Pacific Ocean, from Mexico to Formosa, *except in those waters tributary to the Sea of Japan.* In these waters there is no native representative of the

* *The Origin and Speciation of Oncorhynchus,* by Ferris Neave F.R.S.C., Transactions of the Royal Society of Canada, Vol. LII; Series III; June 1958.

genus *Salmo*. But, limited to them and nearby waters of the Asiatic shore, is the Japanese cherry salmon, *Oncorhyn-chus masou*.

The cherry salmon is an interesting fish. The only specimens I have seen are preserved in a jar in the Institute of Fisheries at the University of British Columbia. They are small fish, not over three or four pounds, and one is immediately impressed by the broad, heavily spotted tails and the thick wrist or caudal peduncle above it. One thinks at once of steelhead or rainbow trout, but the anal fin has the thirteen or more rays typical of *Oncorhynchus* and the fish is, in fact, a Pacific salmon. But it is the most "primitive" type of the genus—that is, the least specialized away from the steelhead or the Atlantic salmon. Dr. Neave notes that it is "piscivorous; lives in both streams and lakes; is also anadromous, but is not far-ranging in its marine habitat; some males, maturing in fresh water, are said to survive after spawning."

The limited distribution of the cherry salmon, and the absence of the steelhead-rainbow group from the same waters, draws attention to the probability of another isolation. Some half a million years ago the land forms near the Japanese Islands rose and cut off the Sea of Japan, forming a shallow, landlocked body of brackish water. The evidence suggests that the steelhead populations trapped under these conditions for thousands of years developed into the cherry salmon. When the ocean waters flooded over again, the cherry salmon were released, only to be trapped again by subsequent rises of the land forms in the Sea of Japan, the Sea of Okhotsk and the Bering Sea. During these later isolations—there may have been more than one—the other five species of Pacific salmon developed from the cherry salmon. With the final flooding in of the ocean, over a hundred thousand years ago, they were released to spread through the range they now occupy.

This is a gross oversimplification of Dr. Neave's most carefully argued paper, but it gives an idea of the biological and geological factors that have almost certainly worked to separate the Atlantic and Pacific types of salmon. Dr. Neave also deals with the difficult question of how the five or six species of Pacific salmon have been able to maintain their evolutionary specialization in spite of the intermingling of stocks almost throughout their range.

It is well known that successful crossbreeding between any of the five North American species can be readily achieved, and that the hybrids are fertile. Yet hybrids are rarely or never found under natural conditions, although the various species are often found spawning in the same areas of the same streams at approximately the same times. Physical differences, though not great in the immature fish, remain constant and the life histories of the five species are widely different and remain so. In other words, the species have developed and are maintaining their development, perhaps increasing it, without the isolation of geographical factors, of different breeding times or of widely differing ecological needs. The species are known to intermingle before they leave fresh water, in their salt-water movements and even at the time of their spawning return.

But although the species are a good deal alike in the silvery coloration and graceful shape of their salt-water forms, they become markedly different in both color and shape with sexual maturity. The sockeye salmon develops

a scarlet body and greenish head, the coho becomes a rich
crimson, often with a black head, the king salmon turns
through bronze to red and black, the pink salmon male
builds a great hump on his back and narrows his body,
the chum salmon develops strong black and gold horizontal
bars which change to red and black vertical barring in
the dominant males. There are other differences, less noticeable to the human eye, but perhaps equally significant.
Dr. Neave suggests that these alterations of shape and color
constitute recognition characteristics to which the breeding fish respond, thus almost entirely preventing inter-
breeding between the species and so providing the necessary "isolation."

There was a long period of time after the subsidence of
the Asiatic land forms in which the five North American
species worked their way around the North Pacific semicircle, and there must also have been withdrawals in the
face of the various ice ages. The present range has been
achieved only since the last retreat of the ice some ten
thousand years ago, and in a more limited form evolution
has continued.

In every river system of any considerable size there are
likely to be several runs or races of fish within each species.
These runs may vary little or much in their timing—from
spring to early fall in the king salmon, for instance, even
on short rivers, and from early July to late September in
the sockeye runs of the Fraser watershed. Runs often vary
in size; and they are usually directed towards different
spawning areas. Because Pacific salmon home faithfully
to the spawning area of their origin, these separate runs
are effectively isolated in their breeding and produce fish

with similar characteristics. There can be little doubt that most such runs developed behind the retreating ice and represent differences in the reserves of energy within the fish themselves on leaving salt water, those stocks with the greatest reserves pushing on to more and more remote spawning areas as the ice withdrew. While it is true that pink and chum salmon, the latter especially, tend to spawn in the lower reaches of streams, and the wing and sockeye go farthest upstream, it is also true that some kings and sockeyes spawn only a short distance above salt water, while some pink salmon travel great distances upstream. In other words, variations in this respect within certain species is almost as great as the widest variation *between* the species.

All this outlines the wonderful complexity of the Pacific salmons and their wide range. They are at once highly specialized to conditions they have accepted and highly adaptable over periods of time to newly favorable conditions that open to them. Sockeye salmon, for instance, are dependent on a year of lake feeding before migrating to sea, and major runs are found only on spawning areas from which the fry can quickly find their way into a lake; yet many streams without accessible lakes have runs of so-called "creek" sockeye—fish that seem to be waiting for some distant chance of geology to open conditions that will permit their increase. The energy reserves of some upstream runs of sockeye are so closely calculated to the distance they must travel that a delay of three days may impair spawning and a delay of twelve days may make it totally ineffective; yet some early king salmon races reach their spawning areas months before they are ripe. The pink salmon completes his whole life history, from egg to death, in two years. The cycle is immutable and total disaster to a given run in a given year should wipe out the run for all time. Yet the pink salmon persists in abundance in many streams, though really large runs are usually in alternate years only.

The coho salmon, which is perhaps closest to the Japanese cherry salmon and through that fish to the steelhead and the Atlantic salmon, spends one year of stream feeding before migration and two years of sea feeding; it spawns and dies nearly always as a three-year-old, though four-year-olds are not unknown and a number of males spawn precociously as two-year-olds. The typical king salmon spends only a month or two in fresh water and returns to spawn in this fourth year; yet some runs are made up almost entirely of five-year-olds. King salmon like large streams with a heavy flow and coarse gravel; the little pink salmon prefers finer gravel and a gentler flow; the coho pushes his way up the smallest streams, through beaver dams and swamps and brush piles; the chum salmon often spawns in water that is still tidal.

No doubt it is scientifically unsound to say that all these runs and races, all these variations of choice and habit and life history were especially designed to use every square yard of accessible stream bed around the perimeter of the North Pacific; it would be sounder to say that the ocean itself and its tributary streams have forced the fish into their present complexity of variation. Yet both points have to be sound in some measure and it is strangely satisfying to think that those thousands of years of species formation in the Japan Sea, the Okhotsk Sea and the Bering Sea eventually led to the miraculous abundance of the Pacific salmon. An abundance such as this could not have been achieved by a single species nor, it would seem, by the several species of the genus *Salmo*. "True salmon" or not—and in the last analysis this is really a matter of individual choice—the Pacific salmon are one of the most useful and impressive wonders of the natural world.

2. *A Word for the Small Streams*

FROM MY OWN PARTICULAR POINT OF view, which is that of a stream fisherman and a fly-fisherman, the Pacific salmons are not ideal game fish. I say this reluctantly and after many years of trying to convince myself otherwise, because they do at times reward the fly-fisherman greatly and under some conditions they give some fine moments of sport in streams. But one has to accept the fact that as fly-rod fish in fresh water they do not rate with the Atlantic salmon, the steelhead or the other true trouts.

In spite of these narrow and personal views, the Pacific salmons make up one of the world's greatest and most exciting sport fisheries. Hundreds of thousands of anglers fish for them season after season, with deepest devotion, and hundreds of thousands of others would like to. They are wise in this because in salt water, and on their own terms, the Pacific salmons are game fish with few equals.

They strike freely, fight at least as well as any other fish of their varying weights and are noble prizes when caught —handsome, shapely and richly fleshed. The coho is the mainstay of the fishery because he is found nearly everywhere, often feeding freely close inshore. He is also the most spectacular performer on the end of a line, running fast and far and jumping with splendid abandon. The king salmon is strength and power, especially when he reaches weights of thirty pounds and over. He feeds deeper and fights deeper than the coho and is often feeding little or not at all as he works towards his rivers from his years of ocean feeding. The little pink salmon often shows up strongly in the sport catch in his high-cycle years and performs worthily enough if the gear is not too heavy. The other two are seldom significant to sportsmen, the sockeye because he is by preference a crustacean feeder and does not often strike at a lure, the chum because he runs late in the year, when few fishermen are out, and does not linger long to be caught.

At first it seems strange that these salmon should make a great salt-water fishery when the Atlantic salmon is rarely fished for or taken with hook and line in salt water. The difference is largely in the numbers of fish, though differences of habit may contribute to some extent. The Atlantic salmon approaches his rivers from a distance and appears to run rather directly into them; many Pacific salmon also return from great distances at sea, but the return is a more leisurely one, with time for feeding on the way; others live what might be called an onshore life, feeding throughout their salt-water years in inside waters like the Gulf of Georgia or along the continental shelf.

These last probably make up the bulk of the rod-fisherman's catch. But even when these differences are allowed for there could be little productive fishing without enormous numbers of fish. Searching the inside waters from Puget Sound to Alaska with rod and line for anything less than runs of commercial magnitude would be as formidable as one of the labors of Hercules.

This establishes the interesting point that the sport fishery is a by-product of the commercial fishery. The sports fisherman, even in his tens of thousands, is not efficient enough to catch more than a small fraction of the numbers his sport depends on. Only the commercial fisherman can justify such numbers by catching them and putting them to use, for there are far more than enough to populate the available spawning areas.

This means that the sport fisherman and the commercial man have a common interest—both can use and profit by more fish. Yet the common interest is often lost sight of in quarrels and arguments about who shall get what fish there are. It is a pity, because all the strength and energy of both sides is needed to preserve the fish and ensure their increase.

Some thirty or forty years ago, the sport fisherman had few problems. Commercial fishing was more localized and not nearly as efficient as it is today. Some runs were hit hard, perhaps overfished, but these were likely to be sockeye or pink runs, usually the former. Most runs were underfished, leaving excessively heavy spawning escapements to the sport fisherman. Truly phenomenal catches were made in those days—ten or more cohos per day on a trolled bucktail fly was not at all unusual, and I have known a single fisherman to take as many as forty.

Catches of this size are more than any sportsman needs or should want, except perhaps once or twice in a lifetime. But a man sitting in a boat with nothing much to do but hang his rod over the side and hope, does need a little action and there is no doubt that catches have now fallen off to the point where he doesn't always get it.

There are many reasons for this. Logging, followed by fires, has silted and severely damaged many streams that produced cohos in good numbers. Nearly all streams are affected in some measure by excessive flooding in winter and low flows in summer after the removal of the trees; some of the smaller streams that formerly produced well for their size now dry up altogether in later summer and so cannot support coho runs. Settlement has contributed to the damage in many places. Pollution has caused some losses, as has the insane practice of removing stream gravel for construction purposes. But in spite of all these injuries, coho salmon continue to run in large numbers and many streams still have what are considered adequate numbers of spawning fish. It is true also that some of the damage is repairing itself as the timber grows back.

I do not in any way want to discount or excuse these abuses. Their cumulative effect is great and there can be no possible doubt that it has made a great difference to the fishery. But it is worth considering another factor—the greatly increased efficiency of the commercial fishery. At the present time there are enough boats and gear in the waters of British Columbia, and presumably in Washing-

ton, Oregon and Alaska as well, to catch every salmon
that swims. This formidable array is, of course, closely
regulated; but the regulations are designed to provide an
adequate spawning escapement, which means in effect the
smallest spawning escapement that will maintain the runs.

There are some powerful arguments against excessive
spawning escapements. One of the least important is that
they waste fish that would otherwise have been put to
economic use. Far more important is the fact that they
overcrowd the spawning gravels to the point that the total
spawning effort is damaged, since the late-running fish
destroy the nests and eggs of early-running fish. This is
undoubtedly so when the escapement is very heavy, but
it probably is not so when the escapement is only mod-
erately in excess of the capacity of the spawning areas. The
point would bear close examination, since it may very well
be that only an excessive spawning escapement can provide the numbers of fish essential to a healthy sport fishery.

Yet another point that would bear close examination is
the responsiveness of various stocks of fish to hook and
line fishing. The most intensive sports-fishing activity is
concentrated in such relatively accessible and sheltered
bodies of water as Puget Sound in Washington and the
Gulf of Georgia in British Columbia. Large numbers of
salmon, especially cohos, live out their entire salt-water
lives in these inside waters and are caught there as feeding
fish. Still larger numbers pass through on their return from
feeding in the open ocean. Since these are on their spawning migration and quite well advanced towards maturity,
it is logical that they should be much less responsive to
lure or bait than more local fish. In tentaitve support of

this possibility, it was noticed that in 1962 an exceptionally large escapement of cohos passing through to the Fraser River had little or no effect on the sport fishery, though commercial boats were taking them by tens of thousands in the same waters.

Both commercial trollers and anglers have long recognized that traveling fish are disinclined to take and both have known times when good concentrations of fish have proved extremely reluctant to strike, even though the nets were taking them freely. If this could be shown to be a matter of individual runs, their origins and ocean feeding habits rather than merely one of mood, there would be an excellent case for selective protection, since it is now well established that rod-caught fish have considerably greater economic value that those taken for purely commercial purposes.

It is neither necessary nor desirable that we should get back to the conditions that made it possible for an angler to take ten or even twenty salmon in a day. But the present catch limit in British Columbia is two salmon of twenty inches or more per day. This is enough for a fly-fisherman working a stream—he has plenty of other things to occupy him besides catching fish. Perhaps it is enough, too, for the man trolling from a boat in salt water, but it suggests a slowish day unless the fish happen to be particularly large. He can look at the scenery, of course, or fiddle with his gear or cut bait or talk to a friend; but it would seem he should have at least the prospect of an occasional day with four or five good fish.

I believe it may be perfectly possible to achieve this in British Columbia if we learn to value and protect our

streams as we should and if we can find the selective key
to keeping excessive commercial pressure off the runs that
contribute most to the sport fishery. Here I should admit
that I am vastly more concerned with the first of these
possibilities than the second. There are scores, if not hundreds of small streams on Vancouver Island alone that
are not producing their proper quotas of coho salmon because of industrial damage, usually logging damage. For
the most part they are small, rocky, mountain streams,
though some flow for a good distance through swampy or
fairly flat land. Their productive capacity in terms of raising coho yearlings varies greatly, as does the extent and
quality of their spawning gravels. But nearly all produce
or have produced coho salmon.

It is difficult to assess the precise value of such streams
in terms of the total salmon return, but creeks that one
can step across at normal flow are known to have returns
of four or five hundred cohos, so the total is certainly
important. There is also a real possibility that their con-
tribution to local runs that live out their sea life within
the limits of the Gulf of Georgia is disproportionately
large, in which case any improvement work would be
highly beneficial to sportsmen.

Under the virgin forest these little streams offered something approaching ideal conditions for spawning salmon
and young fish. The sheltering timber stands gave shade
and relatively low temperatures in summer, delayed snow
melt and controlled the run-off of heavy rains in winter.
The forest floor, piled with dead needles or well covered
by low brush, laced and matted with roots, was practically
impervious to erosion and produced little or no silting.

Roots protected the banks and fallen tree trunks made sheltered rest pools for mature fish and nursing pools for pre-migrants.

Pacific Coast logging through the first fifty years of this century was an affair of heedless devastation. Flats and benches and hill slopes were stripped clear of timber without the slightest consideration for the other values of land or water. Fires usually followed the logging, getting good hold in the waste of limbs and treetops and other debris, and burned the soil to powder. Creeks were filled with trash and logs were dragged across spawning gravels. Sometimes the creeks were robbed of gravel for road building. Perhaps it was all necessary; certainly it was done almost universally, over thousands of square miles of country. If so, the cost was very high, and is still being paid.

After the fires, the rains came, washing the silt of the exposed and burned soil into the streams, clogging the spawning gravels so that water could no longer sift through to carry oxygen to the buried eggs of the salmon. Snow and rain drained off almost as soon as it fell, making short fierce floods through the winters and drought in the summers. There was little shade and little shelter along the unprotected banks of the creeks. No change could have been much more complete and the salmon runs were gravely harmed.

But in time a country recovers, even from such abuse as this. Trees have grown back along many of the creeks, trees and brush again cover many of the hillsides. The soil is again held by the intertwined roots and sheltered from the direct wash of the rain, while the deciduous trees shed their leaves each year to restore some of its virtue. The

creeks flow clean again and more steadily. Some have
washed their gravels clean again, some have not. In some
the salmon have returned to something approaching their
former numbers, in others they have not.

These little streams are valuable. Every one is a potential
salmon producer and nearly every one can be made to produce more fish than it is producing today; many, perhaps
all, can be made to produce more than they did under
primitive conditions.

Five main factors are involved: quality and permeability
of the gravel; stability of stream flow; freedom from obstructions; protected resting water for both mature fish and
fingerlings; adequate nursing shallows for the young fish.
For coho salmon, stability of flow, especially enough flow
in the summer months, is probably the most critical factor,
since the young fish spend a full year of feeding in the
stream before migrating; a very low summer flow will
mean losses through starvation. But all the factors must
be in balance. A good summer flow is of little value if it
is over a bottom so heavily silted that the eggs die for lack
of oxygen and food organisms cannot multiply. Good flow
over good gravel may not be enough to compensate for
heavy losses to predators if there are no protected pools.
And the most perfect stream conditions mean nothing if
access to them is blocked by obstructions or so delayed
that spawning is affected. Excessive floods may be almost
as damaging as very low flows. If they occur at spawning
time the fish will be forced into sheltered places and many
may die without spawning, as was the case with a late run
of dog salmon on the Big Qualicum River, British Columbia, in 1962. If the floods are later they will wash out
gravel and eggs and destroy much of the spawning.

All these five factors and a sixth one, temperature, can be controlled within certain limits. The question of whether or not to undertake control is really a matter of economics—will the increased return of fish pay for the cost of the work within a reasonable space of time? For major works, such as the storage and diversion facilities that may be necessary for full flow control, the answers are not always easy, though they will become so when the results of the experiment on the Big Qualicum River are complete. But for lesser matters such as the improvement of spawning gravels, clearing of silt, removal of obstructions and general improvement of holding and nursing qualities in a stream, the answers should be easily found. By no means all streams need all the different types of attention, but nearly all could be made better producers by a little simple improvement work.

A majority of small spawning streams, for instance, are excessively steep and rapid. Areas of useful water for spawning, nursing and resting could be enormously increased in nearly all of them by "stepping"—that is, by breaking their gradients into flats and little falls with firmly planted cross logs. The initial cost of such work would be very small and its benefits should be large. Some annual maintenance work would be necessary, but so long as the steps were well planned and well constructed in the first instance most of them should last for many years. In some creeks steps of large rocks could be used to good effect.

Streams that are badly silted could be significantly improved by a mobile pump that would pick up the silt and throw it well back from the banks without disturbing the original stream bed. So far as I know, no machine has yet been developed specifically for this purpose, but it certainly would not be hard or costly to put one together. Streams whose beds are unsatisfactory for spawning or rearing purposes could often be improved by the importation of gravel of the right quality from nearby salt-water beaches.

Other possibilities are the restoration of old spawning channels from which the stream has been diverted by obstructions; the opening up of new spawning water by fish passes at falls; the cribbing of cut banks or slides where silting is likely to be caused by flood water; and in some instances it might well be economic to divert a stream from an old, unsatisfactory bed into a well-designed artificial channel.

A practical program of small-stream improvement along these lines could, I believe, be developed without difficulty from present knowledge. It should be a progressive program, starting with a few streams that obviously lend themselves to improvement and developing year by year until every stream is adequately improved, protected and cared for. Present logging practices, especially the replacement of clear cutting by patch logging and other more selective operations, do not cause nearly so much damage as the old ways, and future operations should cause even less. Ground cover of some sort has now restored itself on very large acreages of logged-over land. Both these factors should tend to facilitate improvement work and should reduce maintenance costs as floods become less extreme.

It is reasonable to suppose that the effective spawning area of many small streams could be doubled without great cost, and this is important. But the improvement in rearing capacity through better conservation and distribution of stream flows would be of far greater significance in terms of coho salmon production. Though other factors, such as increased predation, might offset results in some instances, it seems reasonable to suggest that survival from fry to migrant stage could often be increased ten times.

This, then, is my plea for the creeks and little streams. It really asks for nothing more than reasonable care—the sort of care that would be given by any private owner of such a stream. It would not only serve the salmon well, but would also give clear notice to all land and water users and to the public in general that streams are important and valuable assets, not mere accidents of nature.

3. *New Horizons*

I HAVE CHOSEN TO WRITE OF THE CREEKS and little salmon streams as though precise scientific knowledge of their possibilities did not exist. This is a deliberate choice, because I feel that we have quite enough general knowledge to start at once on a useful and economic program of stream rehabilitation and improvement; and I believe, too, that to delay any longer than we already have is both wasteful and dangerous. The expenditure needed for an effective program would not be too great and it might very well lead to more rapid learning by experience than our present rather cautious program of learning by carefully controlled experiments.

There is, in fact, a great deal of extremely advanced experimental salmon work being done on the Pacific Coast. It ranges all the way from selective breeding to stream conditions, from fry survival to spawning mortality, from population dynamics to the energy output of individual fish. There is also a good deal of superbly successful restoration and management of large commercial runs—I am thinking now of the work of the International Pacific Salmon Fisheries Commission on the Fraser River and of the remedial work in progress on the Babine River in the Skeena watershed. But three experiments stand out in their special meaning for small-stream management. These are the Jones Creek, Robertson Creek and Big Qualicum River projects, all in British Columbia; they are so fascinating and their implications are so important that they are of interest to sportsmen everywhere.

Some twenty miles west of Hope, British Columbia, on the TransCanada Highway, there is a bridge over the remnants of Jones Creek. The creek is unmarked and not easy to find, yet it is a famous place—so far as I know, the first successful man-made spawning ground for salmon in the world. Searching for it, I wandered off the highway and along a dirt road, where I found a small boy leaning over a bridge with a fishing rod in his hands. When I asked for Jones Creek he knew nothing of such a stream. But when I described the channel and its use he understood at once.

"Oh, you mean the spawnery. Sure, I know where that is." He gave me exact and detailed directions.

It was just as well he did so, for the "spawnery" does not advertise itself. Jones Creek was originally a lively mountain stream, draining Jones Lake down a steep mountainside, under the highway and then through comparatively flat land for about three-quarters of a mile to the Fraser. In 1953 a high dam was built near the outlet of the lake to direct much of the flow. By 1955 the creek's normal spawning run of five or six thousand humpbacks and a few hundred cohos and dog salmon had fallen off to about four hundred fish. In time even this remnant would probably have been lost.

Some limited flow was made available by passing a single tributary stream around the dam. By itself, this flow would not have been nearly enough to serve the twenty-two hundred square yards of natural spawning area in the bed of Jones Creek, so a special channel was built to make the best possible use of the water.

If you look carefully along the left bank of Jones Creek, in the pool just below the highway bridge, you will find a small diversion valve set in concrete. A few steps below this is a quiet pool of even flow and depth which continues smoothly for a hundred feet or so, then drops over a timber baffle into another similar pool. This is the spawning channel and it continues in this way, between gravel banks that are thickly grown with fresh green alder and over baffles set about a hundred feet apart, for nearly half a mile. To be precise, it is twenty-two hundred feet long and ten feet wide. Its bottom is a layer of gravel twelve to eighteen inches deep, screened to sizes varying from a quarter of an inch to one and a half inches, mixed in proportions then considered satisfactory for spawning humpback salmon. The depth of the water over the channel averages between one and two feet, flowing at a rate of approximately one mile an hour. The whole thing looks like exactly what it is, a tiny idealized stream of perfect proportions. Though on a smaller scale, it reminds me a good deal of the carefully tended chalk stream that flowed through my grandfather's garden in England.

In the fall of 1955 four hundred humpbacks came back to this quiet, protected little stream. They liked it and spawned there. Under natural conditions the survival of their eggs to the fry stage would have been between three and ten per cent, probably more nearly three per cent. In the protection of the man-made spawning channel it was thirty-seven per cent and 160,000 fry left the channel on their seaward migration the following spring.

In 1957 some fifteen hundred adult humpbacks came back to the channel to spawn. Again the survival was high and over 360,000 migrants went down to the Fraser on their way to sea in the spring of 1958. Before the spawning run of 1959 the gravel of the channel was thoroughly cleaned of silt. Twenty-six hundred adults returned from the seeding of 1957 and laid one and a half million eggs. The survival in the freshly cleaned gravel reached the astonishing figure of sixty-three per cent and nearly a million fry started seaward the following spring. Over five thousand of these came back to spawn in 1961. In just six years, three cycles, the run had built almost to its previous maximum. The run of 1963 will certainly exceed it.

Jones Creek is a very small project; its capital cost was just over $60,000 and maintenance costs through six years of operation have been about $10,000. It has dealt with the simplest of all the salmons, the little humpback whose two-year life history yields quick results and whose fresh-water needs are limited to the spawning and hatching processes, since the fry migrate to salt water as soon as they have absorbed the last of their yolk sacs and are able to swim freely. But it emphasizes as almost nothing else could the enormous part played in survival rates by two factors—the stream flow and the quality of the spawning gravel. Under the controlled conditions, there is no possibility of losses through heavy flooding or drying out of the beds. The gravel is clean and of good size and depth to allow a proper flow of water around the eggs during the hatching period. While some silting does occur, it can be cleaned out periodically at reasonable cost.

It was obvious that these principles could be expanded and applied to other species—chum salmon spawning in the Jones Creek channel achieved a survival rate of thirty per cent, even though the channel was not designed specifically for their needs. Experience at Jones Creek also suggested that the gravel sizes chosen were not ideal and that some modification of gradients might improve the effective flow of oxygen-bearing water through the gravel.

The Robertson Creek project, on Vancouver Island, was a direct development from Jones Creek, with at least some encouragement from the reported success of a man-made spawning channel built below the McNary Dam, on the Oregon side of the Columbia River, in 1957. Robertson Creek was originally an overflow outlet from Great Central Lake into the Stamp River, carrying a stream only at times of high water. A logging control dam built at the main outlet of the lake in 1923 raised the lake level sufficiently to permit a continuous flow; minor runs of coho and spring salmon established themselves in the limited spawning area of the creek between then and 1957, when a more permanent dam was built. At the same time a control dam was built at Robertson Creek.

The project started out with two important advantages: a substantial controlled flow of water was available and the water itself, drawn from the lower end of a large lake, carried little or no silt. The natural stream bed of the creek offered a good line for the spawning channel, though its gradient was rather too steep. The steepness has been broken by a series of weirs, called "drop structures," which are simply a more sophisticated version of the wooden baffles separating the pools at Jones Creek.

The channel at Robertson Creek is about the same length as the one at Jones Creek, but its width is thirty-five feet instead of ten feet, giving it about three and a half times the spawning area of Jones Creek. The normal flow is about eighteen inches deep at a speed of one mile an hour. The most important difference between the two channels is in the size of the gravel selected for Robertson Creek. Jones Creek gravel, screened to a maximum of one and a half inches, had shown a tendency to pack and lose permeability rather rapidly. Robertson Creek gravel varies from three-quarters of an inch to four inches.

While the Jones Creek project was conceived for a specific purpose, the restoration of an individual salmon run, Robertson Creek is both more ambitious and more broadly experimental. In addition to the artificial spawning channel it has a series of rearing ponds and a test flume for study of the energy output of migrating fish and experiments in the diversion of downstream migrants. A trap and elevator at the outlet of the channel make it possible to select spawners and transport them to the proper sections of the channel or into the lake itself if they are not needed. The rearing ponds are of particular interest to sports fishermen, since they can be used to determine the exact quantity of natural flow needed to raise coho and steel-head pre-migrants through their fresh-water years. Results should have important bearing on stream-improvement projects.

The spawning channel at Robertson Creek at present has two assignments, to increase the small natural spawning runs of spring and coho salmon and to establish a humpback salmon run in the watershed. Since humpback runs are generally very light all along the west coast of Vancouver Island and none at all had been known to exist in the upper reaches of the Somass river system, to which Robertson Creek is tributary, this last was an important test.

The first planting of humpback eggs in the channel was in 1959. Less than two million eggs were available instead of the six or eight million the experiment called for, but the ideal conditions produced an unheard-of survival of well over ninety per cent, and over a million and a half fry went down the river in the spring of 1960. The return of adults from these in 1961 was insignificant, though there were unconfirmed reports of humpbacks showing in unusual numbers at various points in Barclay Sound, the arm of the sea into which the Somass system drains. But as I write this, in the fall of 1963, seven thousand adult humpbacks have come back to the Robertson Creek channel to spawn and others may be following them. This in itself is a spectacular success, because it means that an entirely new run has been established and it seems to mean, too, that there is nothing inherently unfavorable to humpback salmon in sea conditions on the west side of the Island. Although humpbacks normally run strongly to any given stream only in alternate years, a substantial planting of eggs from the Atnarko River was made at Robertson Creek in 1962; and if the fall of 1964 brings a substantial return, another important question will have been answered.

It is not necessary to labor the implications of this kind of work. Robertson Creek is an outdoor laboratory equipped to conduct research that has direct application to natural conditions. The next step beyond it has already been taken in the Big Qualicum project, also on Vancouver Island. Here an attempt is being made to bring an entire watershed under full control for the benefit of anadromous fish—and the benefit of both commercial and sports fishermen.

Big Qualicum River, in spite of its name, is a small stream flowing into the Gulf of Georgia on the east side of Vancouver Island. The total area of the watershed, most of which drains into Horne Lake, is fifty-eight square miles. From the lake the river flows eight miles to the sea.

This stretch of river supports average annual runs of thirty-five thousand dog salmon, thirty-five hundred cohos, a thousand kings, a few humpbacks and good numbers of cutthroat and steelhead trout. The stream is subject to wide variations of flow, from about seven thousand cubic feet a second in flood time to a minimum of only fifteen cubic feet a second in some spawning seasons. Hunts Creek, the only significant tributary below the lake, has an even wider fluctuation and is subject to flash flooding. It is easy to understand that extremes of this sort can do a great deal of damage to spawning areas and cause heavy losses of eggs and fry. Low summer flows also limit the stream's potential for rearing young cohos and steelheads, since these fish spend one and two years respectively in fresh water before going to sea.

Expressed simply, the purpose of the Big Qualicum project is to bring the entire watershed under control and distribute the run-off evenly throughout the year, so that the lower seven miles of stream bed, which supports all the migratory runs, will have a stable and adequate flow. The first step was the diversion of Hunts Creek into a flood channel that carries surplus flow to a point just above tidewater, where a large concrete drop structure prevents the upstream passage of fish. While this represents some wastage of flow and spawning area, control would have been disproportionately expensive. It will still be possible to bring the creek under control when the results of the main project are fully known.

The key to the main project is in Horne Lake, which has a surface area of three square miles. A small dam, built at the lake's natural outlet, provides storage to twenty-eight feet above the former level. By itself, this is not enough to provide full control. Immediately below the outlet of the lake is a three-quarter mile stretch of canyon in which the river drops nearly two hundred feet. By drilling back from the foot of this canyon through the base of a rocky hill, it has been possible to tap the lake at a point seventy feet below its normal level, thus giving a total storage range of ninety-eight feet. Water is released through this intake into an eight-foot tunnel which carries it through two thousand feet of rock back to the foot of the canyon. The intake is designed to draw water from three different levels, twenty, forty and eighty feet below the normal lake level, which permits temperature control over a range of five degrees centigrade during the critical spawning months.

These works are designed to give an even flow of about

two hundred cubic feet a second through the natural stream bed, day in, day out through twelve months of the year. They will eliminate all losses and damage through flooding or drying out of the spawning areas and in theory should increase the stream's capacity for raising coho and steelhead pre-migrants by about fourteen times. In scale comparison with Robertson Creek, Big Qualicum gives twice the flow over fourteen times the distance, though the natural stream bed cannot be expected to give the same high survival rates as Robertson Creek's selected gravel. However, the natural stream bed can be improved and there is plenty of room in the valley floor for the construction of supplementary artificial channels.

Though it is essentially experimental, since nothing just like it has been attempted before, and its results, which will be intensively observed, should have important bearing on future stream improvement plans, the Big Qualicum project has a direct economic purpose. Total cost of the project has been about one and a quarter million dollars, which compares with about a quarter of a million dollars for Robertson Creek. The reasonable expectation is that under controlled flow conditions the stream should bring spawning returns at least as large as the largest previously recorded. In the case of the dog salmon runs alone, this amounts to one hundred thousand fish. Annual returns of this order would pay for the project through increased commercial yields within fifteen years. But the calculated capacity of the seven miles of natural stream bed would allow successful spawning of two hundred thousand fish. With only limited improvement of the natural channel, through screening and cleaning of the gravel, escapements of this order may be expected. If achieved, they will increase the annual commercial catch of dog salmon from the watershed to at least four hundred thousand fish, compared to the former average of seventy. thousand. The difference represents, at present values, an increase in landed value of $330,000 a year.

Besides this, roughly equivalent increases in size can be expected for the present runs of kings, cohos, cutthroat and steelhead trout. It is also hoped that the small existing run of pink salmon may respond to reduced spawning temperatures and a short artificial spawning channel just above the present counting fence.

Big Qualicum project was completed in time for the fall runs of 1962. Ironically, on a watershed dedicated entirely to fisheries management, it still ran into conflict with electric power. An important power line passes along one side of Horne Lake and when the lake was drawn down below its normal level one of the pylons was undermined by springs and collapsed. Since then the inimitable ineptitudes of government bureaucracies have managed to keep anything at all from being done. The power line has to be relocated, of course, and at considerable expense, but not all the Queen's horses and all the Queen's men of the provincial and federal governments combined have so far been able to accept the idea and get busy on it. Meanwhile Horne Lake must be maintained within its normal levels, which permit only a few feet of storage. Floods in the 1962-63 winter caused major spawning losses and it is by no means certain that control will be possible in the 1963-64 season.*

* Control was established in November 1963.

Even government departments, fortunately, are seldom able to keep things permanently fouled up and it seems likely that full draw-down of Horne Lake should become possible within a few more months at most. It is impossible to doubt that the project will be successful; the really dramatic element is in the degree of success that may be achieved. If anything approaching the improvements I have suggested above are realized, the way will be open for a whole series of similar undertakings which could, in a comparatively short while, build salmon and steelhead runs to a point well beyond their greatest natural abundance.

No doubt other limiting factors are bound to enter sooner or later to keep this fisherman's dream within bounds. But I am optimistic enough to believe that the North Pacific Ocean can grow a lot more salmon than are using it now; and I hope I shall live long enough to see its capacity become a question of immediate moment.

4. *Pacific Salmon in Salt Water*

SOME FORM OF TROLLING IN SALT WATER is and always has been overwhelmingly the most effective means of catching Pacific salmon for sport. Trolling is also a highly effective means of commercial fishing, accounting for about seventy per cent of the total British Columbia king salmon catch, or half a million fish, and sixty per cent of the coho catch or rather over two million fish, in an average season. The catch of salmon by sportsmen is usually between three and four hundred thousand a year, roughly ten per cent of the total troll catch for the province; but most of the sport fishery is concentrated in the general area around the shores of the Gulf of Georgia, and here sport fishing accounts for about thirty-five per cent of the troll catch.

During the past twenty years, sport fishermen have increased enormously in numbers and their equipment has become much more formidable. With outboard motors and planing hulls, distant fishing grounds have suddenly become close; trailers to transport the boats by road and small cabin cruisers extend the range still further. Yet the salt-water salmon fisherman today is scratching for fish as he rarely had to in the 1930's. Nothing emphasizes this so plainly as do the changes in gear and fishing methods.

There were outboards, of course, in the 1930's, but they were relatively few and none too reliable; they drove simple rowboats with displacement hulls that could not make more than six or seven miles an hour. Most sport fishermen rowed when fishing, even though they might run to the grounds by motor. Favorite lures for cohos were small bright spoons, small plugs and large hair wet flies with silver bodies. It was seldom necessary to use more than two ounces of lead and as often as not one could fish the lure right at the surface, with no weight at all. When conditions were right, some fishermen tied up or drifted and cast herring strip and even flies with good effect. For spring salmon, larger plugs and spoons were popular and slightly heavier weights were used. Trolling or casting with herring strip was popular and a few fishermen "mooched" —that is, drifted their boats through likely places, with only guiding movements of the oars, fishing whole herring, herring plug or strip as near bottom as possible. Catches of six or eight cohos or two or three kings on a tide were not at all unusual.

All these methods still catch fish today, sometimes as well as ever; mooching and strip-casting remain, for skillful fishermen, among the most effective methods under a wide variety of conditions. But the average troller, which means most salt-water salmon fishermen, no longer puts his trust in the simplicity of small spoons and plugs fished close to the surface. Fish are not found so easily now and he must look harder for them, with more complicated and less attractive methods.

Fishing tackle of all types is almost constantly improving and improvements have been particularly great over the past twenty years. No one has benefited more than the salt-water salmon fisherman. The perfection of the glass rod has given him a wide choice of excellent rods at reasonable prices. He can safely use, and generally does use, a light and flexible rod of good length instead of the short, heavy wood or cane rods that were formerly popular. A wide choice of good reels, from large capacity fixed spools to star drag multipliers, is also available; and if prices are sometimes rather high he can always fall back on the best reel of all for his purpose, the single-action Nottingham type which is now made of various synthetic materials. Nylon monofilament makes an excellent salt-water line, impervious to rot, not too much given to kinking, available in every conceivable thickness and strength, and cheap. True, nylon can be a trap for the careless or unwary fisherman. It is tricky to knot, cuts or cracks rather easily and often breaks unaccountably, but these faults do not outweigh its advantages. In the larger sizes, twenty-pound breaking strain and up, it shows in the water like a quarter-inch cable under certain light conditions, a factor that may well be more disturbing to the fish than it seems to be to most fishermen. However that may be, it is almost universally preferred today for both lines and leaders. Properly tied, nylon in good condition is practically unbreakable, even in the finer sizes, because of its elasticity.

The modern outboard motor, besides getting the fisherman quickly and easily to more distant fishing grounds, runs well and fairly quietly at trolling speeds. This is an important advantage in fishing for coho, since these fish usually take best at a speed somewhat faster than most of us care to row. Outboard enthusiasts often defeat their own purpose by running enthusiastically from place to place instead of settling down to a sensible period of serious fishing, but there is no doubt that, on the balance, fishermen can fish more hours, in better places and more efficiently with motors than with oars.

The postwar years have also brought an enormous increase in the number of well-designed lures. Fortunately there is no such thing as the perfect lure that will take fish at all times, under all conditions, and presumably there never will be; but some of the postwar offerings of the tackle dealers, such as the Norwegian Gresvig Crocodile spoon, are a lot closer to it than anything that was available before, and the range of plugs and wobblers and spinners is enough to give both fish and fishermen every conceivable choice and temptation. Even the flies have been improved, at least for trolling purposes, by the addition of a second hook and heavy wings of long, bright bear fur that give a good action at high speed.

But all these improvements together—and many of them are real improvements that certainly increase the efficiency of the fisherman's effort—have not been enough to produce good fishing. The surest proof of this is in the overwhelming popularity of herring—fresh, frozen or salt—over lures of any kind.

The herring is, of course, an obvious natural bait, either

for king salmon or cohos, since both fish feed freely on
the herring schools in the later stages of their salt-water
life. But it is a great deal more trouble to fish with herring
than with artificial lures. First of all one has to get them—
by jigging or raking for them or by purchase. They may
or may not be the right size or in the right stage of freshness. They must be cut properly and mounted properly
on the tackle, to spin or to wobble if one is trolling, to stir
convincingly in the current if one is mooching.

The next step is to put the herring in the water and hope
it will catch a fish. It probably will. Dogfish, ling cod and
several other fish like herring very well and strike at it
freely. So the cutting and baiting process may have to be
done all over again. Or perhaps a salmon will make a pass
at the herring and strike short. Sometimes he gets the
herring to keep, sometimes he just roughs it up; in either
case the cutting and baiting are to be done again. In addition,
a whole herring or cut herring plug is heavy and awkward
to cast, it becomes soggy and unattractive fairly quickly
and is quite likely to be damaged or torn away if one hooks
weeds or bottom. I mention these assorted shortcomings
with no thought of suggesting that herring is not a good
bait. It is excellent. But if artificial lures would catch fish
as they were catching them twenty years ago, I am sure
that few fishermen would bother with herring; and it is
not that the salmon have changed their habits, only that
they have become fewer where the sport fisherman must
look for them.

Even the informed and skillful use of herring has not
proved enough to produce satisfactory catches, so many
fishermen have chosen to inflict upon themselves an ultimate horror—the "flasher" or "attractor" or "dodger." This

is an enormous piece of bright metal, sometimes as much as
eighteen inches long by three or four inches wide, shaped
more or less like a spoon. It is attached to the line a few feet
above the lure or bait and in this position is dragged
through the water. Its primary purpose is to send a bright
flash to a considerable distance through the water and so
draw the salmon over to investigate. In the course of his
investigations he is likely to come upon the lure or herring
that is trailing behind and take appropriate action. A secondary purpose may be to impart some subtly different
action to the lure or bait. Some fishermen believe that the
flasher suggests another feeding salmon in action and so
stimulates the competitive instincts of the real fish, some
feel that it looks like herring or other feed, some that it
gets its results simply by suggesting some sort of underwater activity.

Flashers are ugly, clumsy and awkward to fish with.
They put a heavy drag on a rod and call for a heavy
tension on the reel. They get in the way in the last stages,
when a fish is being brought to the net and, most serious
of all, they grossly inhibit the activity of the fish when it
is hooked. A good-sized flasher dampens the speed and
efforts of a ten- or fifteen-pound fish to feebleness and
renders a five-pounder practically powerless. It is logical
to assume that no fisherman in his right mind is going to
ruin his sport in this way unless he feels that he must to get
any results at all. And it is certain that flashers do, under
some conditions, make the difference between catching
fish and not catching them. Twenty years ago they were
practically unknown; today they are used most of the time
by a great many fishermen.

Much of what I have written here is from broad observation rather than direct personal experience. One cannot help noticing the tourist boats as they come in with their gear and their few fish; one notices the different preparations of guides and resort owners, listens in the tackle stores and notes the changes on their shelves; one weighs the accounts of the outdoor writers in newspapers and magazines and the altered concerns of trusted and experienced friends. The inevitable conclusion is that a once great fishery has gone a long way down and is still going down. It is not because there are so many more fishermen —there is still water in plenty for all and not so long ago there would have been fish in plenty for all. But now the fish are too few and the fisherman must turn to clumsier and more awkward methods of search for them. In doing so he inevitably reduces the sport still further.

It is important to realize that this is a broad generalization. There is still much good fishing to be found. There are still times when the cohos come eagerly to the fly fished close under the surface, there are still days when a small bright spoon and a half-ounce weight will find more fish than the best cut herring plug weighed down with two or four ounces; there could well be more of them if fishermen found faith again and ventured to try the old ways more often. Certainly there are days and places where the results show plainly that a big flasher finds fish where lesser lures do not, but there are other days and other places, perhaps more of them, where the results show it is merely a useless drag on the line.

I hope I have not suggested any deep-seated contempt for fishing with natural herring. It is a skillful, fascinating and time-honored business. I have often found pleasure in mooching a well-cut herring plug with oars, not a motor,

I admit; it tends to be a slowish form of sport, but it has the fascination of tempting the unknown depths. I have immensely enjoyed casting narrow, lively, fresh-cut strips from a herring's side for feeding cohos and kings. In some ways it is better and more interesting sport than trying to work a fly under the same conditions, because one has far better control of depth and movement. Herring strip is not so popular now as it used to be. "They want the whole herring," fishermen tell me. Perhaps. But there are still times when the strip will find fish and take them.

I am convinced that the only thing that can restore the sport to its former splendor is more fish, and I am equally convinced that it is perfectly possible to have more fish. To a certain extent the sport fisherman is probably spoiling his own sport by taking almost two hundred thousand grilse a year, mainly in Gulf of Georgia waters. Grilse are small salmon of three pounds or less, usually kings or cohos in their first salt-water year. Their growth rate is rapid and their survival rate is high, so that a good proportion of them would show up in the catch of adult salmon if they were left alone.

To a certain extent, too, the commercial effort permitted by the present regulations may be excessive, especially in the Gulf of Georgia. Regulation aims only to ensure the minimum spawning escapement that will properly seed the beds; it is probable that satisfactory sport fishing calls for the maximum escapement that can be allowed without damage through overcrowding of the spawning areas. A spell of lively fishing during the summer of 1963, when a three-week commercial strike permitted a large escapement of humpbacks and cohos, confirms this impression.

But restrictive regulations alone will never make a great

fishery on the scale of today's demand. Only an ambitious and intensive program of stream improvement can achieve this. There should come a day, not too long from now, when every stream in the province is controlled and cared for and guarded as the enormously valuable asset it is. And when that day does come the fisherman will again find his fish with small light lures fished near the surface and take them on gear that allows them to show their proper performance.

5. *Pacific Salmon in Fresh Water*

I HAVE WRITTEN MANY TIMES, WITH EN-
thusiasm, of fishing for Pacific salmon in fresh water. It is
true that the opportunities are limited compared to the
opportunities of salt-water fishing; Pacific salmon do not
rate with either Atlantic salmon or steelhead as fresh-water
game fish. Generally speaking, they run too late and too
close to their spawning and their taking moods are too
uncertain to make for first-class sport. Yet there are many
exceptions to these generalizations; in certain waters and
at certain rather precise times Pacific salmon do give excellent sport in fresh water.

At present it is legal to fish for king and coho salmon in
fresh water; sockeye, pink and chum salmon are not classi-
fied as game fish and are protected. Many sports fishermen
feel that kings and cohos should have similar protection.
Essentially this is an illogical position since many of the
same fishermen fish for steelhead in the rivers and would

unhesitatingly fish for Atlantic salmon if they had the opportunity. It would be just as logical to bar the taking of maturing salmon in salt water by sports fishermen, since nearly all the fish so caught are taken after they have survived the dangers of salt water and are nearing their streams; a mature salmon taken in Cowichan Bay or Comox Harbor or at the head of Howe Sound is just as effectively removed from seeding the redds as though he were taken from actual spawning water. The fresh-water fisherman is, in fact, able to do less damage since his fish are considerably less likely to respond to fly or lure.

Unhappily the present situation is not quite so simple as this. A great many so-called fishermen do go out along the rivers with the deliberate intention of snagging salmon and they are quite successful, either with weighted lures or bare hooks. Sometimes they simply want the fish or the excitement of hooking into something big; but most have a considerably more offensive purpose—they want the eggs of the ripe females for trout or steelhead fishing. This unpleasant practice is likely to increase rather than decrease as time goes on, and it can cause significant losses.

There are regulations against snagging salmon, but they are by no means easy to enforce. A few of the operators take chances and use gear that is obviously designed for the purpose—large treble hooks weighted with lead; one finds the evidence in tackle left on the bottom of the river. But most snaggers make at least some pretense of fishing legally. The usual method is to cast a lure well across a likely reach of river, let it sink, then reel in, reefing violently on the rod top at every few turns. If questioned the "fisherman" merely says that he felt something and was

striking to it; if he is caught as he is about to beach a
snagged fish he has only to deplore the accident and let
the fish go. Conscience in the matter or concern for the
salmon is nonexistent.

Last fall I spent a little while watching a succession
of snaggers at work on a large concentration of pink
salmon just off the mouth of a small creek. Considering
how tightly the fish were schooled and the numbers that
were there, the results were not impressive; certainly no
great harm was done although the performance went on
day after day, because there were more than enough fish
for the capacity of the creek. But it was interesting to see
how calmly and openly these poachers went about their
business. In the end I asked one old fellow who was more
persistent and rather more successful than the average if he
knew that what he was doing was against the law.

"Sure I know it," he said. "But I've tried to catch the
sons-a-bitches every other way, so what's a guy to do?"

In spite of this, I don't think there are many fishermen
who would stand up and openly defend snagging as a sport-
ing way of catching fish and I am satisfied it cannot be
tolerated if the salmon runs are to be maintained. But I
certainly do not think the proper answer is to rule all
anglers off the streams when the salmon are running, as has
been done on occasion. Some of the very best cutthroat and
summer steelhead fishing is to be found at such times and
the few salmon that are taken in fresh water by legitimate
angling give far more interesting and exciting sport than
do salmon taken in salt water. The first step should be to
remove the main cause of the destruction by barring the
use of salmon roe as bait at any time. The second step

should be to limit anglers on salmon streams to the use of unweighted flies and lures with single hooks no larger than No. 2 from July first to November thirtieth. The very few fish that could be snagged on such tackle as this would be insignificant—in fact anyone who really wanted fish would find it more profitable to spend his time fishing for them than trying to snag them.

In spite of the numbers in which they run and the infinite variety of delightful streams to which they run, surprisingly little is understood about the fresh-water response of Pacific salmon to various forms of angling. One can make the broad generalization that they are not very responsive and that this is why more is not known or understood; anglers have accepted defeat and turned to more profitable fields. But any such easy generalization as this must immediately recognize a wide range of interesting and sometimes spectacular exceptions. I am fully prepared to discourage any angler who is planning to come from a distance in the hope of finding good sport with Pacific salmon in fresh water; but I think those of us who live close by good salmon streams owe it to ourselves as anglers to give a good deal more thought and at least a little more action towards understanding the puzzle.

I have written elsewhere of the variation between the species in fresh-water response, suggesting somewhat tentatively that it may be related to the length of fresh-water life before migrating to sea. Both steelhead and Atlantic salmon are likely to spend two years in fresh water and both take comparatively freely on their return. Of the Pacific salmon, both coho and sockeye normally spend one full year in fresh water before migrating; the coho takes most freely of all the species when he is in fresh water again, while the sockeye takes only rarely, but this difference may well be related to the sockeye's pre-migrant habit of feeding exclusively on minute crustaceans. After the coho, the king salmon is probably the most willing taker on his return to fresh water, and he normally spends from two or three months to a full year in river feeding before going to sea.

This again is a broad generalization, with exceptions enough to limit its value to very little. The pink salmon starts down to sea as soon as he is free of his yolk sac; he could be said to have no fresh-water life at all. In some streams you may fish a fly over hundreds of pink salmon, season after season, without the slightest risk of having one take it, and even a spinner or lure will be scarcely more productive. In other streams, often nearby, one may find pink salmon taking so freely that they are a nuisance in some seasons. I have never yet been able to develop even a tentative theory to cover this, yet there must be an explanation of some sort. Temperature, stream flow, the type of holding water and even the chemical values of the water may be involved.

It is quite clear that coho and king salmon jacks—that is, precociously mature male fish returning to spawn after only one year in salt water—take somewhat more freely than full-grown members of the same species. I have, for instance, taken half a dozen coho jacks from a pool before stirring one full-grown fish. This roughly matches the responsiveness of Atlantic salmon grilse and suggests that these fish return to fresh-water habits more readily after their short sea life.

I have caught full-grown coho salmon in fresh-water
pools when they were so newly in from the sea that evidence of salt-water feeding was still plain in their stomachs;
I have caught occasional worn-out spawners as late as February when searching for steelhead, and I have caught them
at every stage between these two extremes. Fresh-run cohos,
on the whole, are likely to be fairly responsive; but I suspect, rather strongly, that the runs of fish most likely to
take in fresh water are those which spend the longest time
in fresh water before spawning. A few streams have runs
that start in mid-June and these always serve the fresh-
water fisherman well. In one northern stream I have caught
cohos over two hundred miles from salt water in mid-
August and suspect that the peak of the run, which arrives
about a month later and takes quite freely, may enter fresh
water before the end of August.

One of the most unusual runs I know comes to a small
lake on the west side of Vancouver Island, twenty-five miles
and sixteen hundred feet in elevation from salt water, by
the first week of August. The lake is about one and a half
miles long by half a mile at its widest, set close in under
the high mountains. A fair stream comes in at the head
over a wide gravel bar, but no fish move into the stream
until the heavy rains come in late September or early
October. They hold in the lake, rolling and splashing on
its quiet surface among the little islands and straight out
from the gravel bar.

For practical purposes the lake, still well back in the
virgin timber, is accessible only by air. But it is fished quite
often during the six or eight weeks the fish are there

because it is an easy place to drop into for an hour or two and the gravel bar is a good place to beach a plane and a pleasant spot to fish from. I am in no position to say that the fish take readily because I have never myself done well there, though I have tried it several times. But I have seen some excellent catches that were made with both spinner and fly from the gravel bar and have heard of many others. As nearly as I can judge, the fish have short and unpredictable taking periods that continue until they move up into the streams to spawn, though with decreasing intensity.

I know of no other run just like this and find myself wondering how it has developed. There are several miles of good spawning water above the lake, but they are probably not highly productive of feed for young fish, so it is likely that the fry drop down to the lake quite quickly and spend most of their first year there. The lake may also be the key to the early return of the adult fish, since it provides excellent shelter and protection with favorable temperatures. These points suggest that the run may be quite a large one in proportion to the size of the stream and also that the responsiveness of the adult fish to flies and lures may reflect their pre-migrant lake-feeding experience.

I do not mean to suggest by these references to "feeding" that the adult coho salmon, or any other salmon or fully grown steelhead for that matter, does actually feed on its return to fresh water. They do not need to, because their bodies carry enough stored fats and oils to carry them through the migration and the spawning act; and they could not feed effectively because the waters they return to have no resources of food that could possibly support them—summer steelhead, for instance, hold over for six months or longer in mountain spawning streams that do not even carry enough food to raise their fry to migrant size. Finally, there is a marked contraction of the stomach in salmon and most steelhead approaching maturity, as well as sharp changes of physiological structure that rule out the possibility of normal function.

But this lack of feeding function in mature salmon and steelhead does not entirely rule out feeding response. Any fisherman who regularly checks the stomachs of the steelhead he catches, for instance, will sooner or later find evidence of this in the shape of occasional stonefly nymphs, salmon eggs, pieces of stick, preened-out duck feathers and other drifting debris. These occasional items, useful or useless, always reflect something readily available at the time, creatures or things that drift to the fish without any effort on his part; although he does not need them, and probably cannot use them, their nearness and availability break through the changes of his mature condition and stir again the reaction to strike that has served him all through his life. It is this highly uncertain response that the fresh-water salmon fisherman is trying to stir.

It might be expected that the fish would respond most readily to echoes of their recent sea experience—rather large, bright spoons or spinners or plugs suggesting the herring and other small fish they had been feeding on. To some limited extent, this is the case, but generally it is small and not particularly bright lures that produce the best results. Cohos often take quite small flies and very small spinners. I remember meeting one man on the Campbell River who had had the hooks broken away from five fly-rod flatfish in succession by king salmon of thirty pounds or more and who was even then hooked into a sixth fish which finally broke his line. Conceivably the very small flatfish echoed the appearance and action of the Euphausiid shrimps that are a favorite salt-water food of king salmon. But it is at least equally possible that the response is conditioned in some way by the fresh-water surroundings—by the different appearance of things in the water or by the reversion of the fish to its pre-migrant fresh-water experience. This last was once suggested to me by the late E. R. Hewitt as a factor in the fresh-water response of Atlantic salmon to artificial nymphs and floating flies. I have taken several coho salmon on nymphlike wet flies and only one on a floating fly, though I have risen at least half a dozen others; since I do not deliberately fish for cohos with either nymphs or floating flies, all these results have come while fishing for steelhead or cutthroat trout, which seems to give them some additional significance. Summer steelhead, of course, take floating flies extremely well under the right conditions.

There is reason enough, I am satisfied, to consider fishing for Pacific salmon, especially cohos, in fresh water a worthwhile sport that should be protected and further developed. The opportunities are not ideal, because in many streams the main run of cohos only enters fresh water a week or two before the fish are ready to spawn and the angler is no longer interested. But even these streams have a scattering of early fish if one can find them, and one fish taken from one's feet with light gear in a good strong stream is worth a dozen taken by trolling a herring and flasher behind an outboard motor. It is unfortunately true that a small lure or spinner will almost invariably take fish far better than a fly of any kind, but in spite of this I do not think the possibilities of fly-fishing for cohos in streams have been very thoroughly explored. There could still be some surprising rewards for careful fly-fishing, especially in streams that have good early runs.

6. *Big Fish and Fresh Water*

T HE WORLD'S RECORD ROD-CAUGHT SAL-
mon is a Pacific king of ninety-two pounds taken in the
Skeena River on July 19, 1959. The fish was over fifty
miles from the sea and the man who caught it, Heinz
Wichmann, was casting from the bank with twenty-five-
pound monofilament line and a comparatively small lure.
The previous world's record dates back to 1910 when
Frank Steele killed an eighty-three-pound fish of the same
species in the Umpqua River in Oregon. The fact that
both these enormous fish were taken in rivers is impressive,
since there must be hundreds, if not thousands, of king
salmon taken by anglers in salt water for every one taken
in fresh; but I would not suggest that fishermen in search
of new world records should confine their attention to
fresh water.

The Skeena at Terrace is a very large river and, like all
large rivers, it must be rather discouraging to fish. But

king salmon like big rivers and it is not unreasonable to
suppose that the best chance of finding really big kings is
in or near the largest rivers. It seems reasonable, too, to
expect the more northerly streams, up to a point, to produce the largest fish; northern fish have a slower growth
rate, but they tend to compensate for this by extra years
of sea feeding. While there are several streams in British
Columbia, from Rivers Inlet north to the Nass and the
Skeena, that might produce a new record fish, the chances
are that the first rod-caught hundred-pounder will come
from Alaska. There are bigger salmon swimming every
year than have yet been brought to beach or boat by rod
and line.

Very big fish are one of the authentic excitements of
salmon fishing. The smaller fish may, and often do, fight
faster, harder and better, but there is something formidable
in the massive power of a salmon of over thirty pounds—
a ponderous authority that increases noticeably with every
additional five or ten pounds of weight. When a hooked
fifty- or sixty-pounder rolls at the surface, he does so with
a majestic slowness that utterly disregards any restraint of
the line; when he breaks water, it is with a violence of
sound and spray that no lesser fish can achieve; when he
decides to run, his determination vibrates through the rod
into the fisherman's arms. At the end, when his rushes are
short, power is still in them; and when at last he turns on
his side or rolls over in exhaustion, sheer weight is still a
threat to tackle and an experienced fisherman knows the
sharpest anxiety of all.

I have yet to beach a sixty-pound salmon and now, considering how seldom I expose myself to the risk of hooking

such a monster, it is not too likely that I ever shall. But if the unlikely should happen, I hope the end of the affair will come towards dusk of a summer evening, near the tail of a big pool on a big river, in shallow water with the current marking the surface no more than enough to stir the late, reflected light. I hope I shall be alone in those last moments when the great gleaming back is breaking the surface, and I hope I shall release the fish to go on to his spawning.

The finest fishing I have ever had for really big king salmon has all been in the farthest tidal pool upstream in the Nimpkish River on Vancouver Island and practically every fish I have caught there has taken a large wobbling spoon fished slow and deep. I have tried a fly through the pool from time to time, but the only success it ever brought me was an occasional coho, though I know now that I did not give it a proper chance. I am pretty sure there are times in that pool, well on in the evening and with the tide ebbing, when the big fish would come to a deep fly.

For the past few years my only opportunity for experimenting with big king salmon has been on the Campbell, not the Nimpkish. The Campbell's mouth has been given over to log booming ever since I have known it and its last good tidal pool is continually disturbed by the dumping of logs, so the fish never lie there well. Less than two miles of river above tidewater are open to the fish and they come into it first early in August. By the first week of September they are dark. By mid-October most are spawning and by the end of November all are dead or dying.

The fish that move in during August are superb creatures, massive and full of strength though turning slightly towards bronze from their ocean silver. Many, it appears, are not

yet fully committed to fresh water and move out again—
certainly the upriver pools are often empty of them after
holding scores of fish a day or two earlier. These August
fish seemed to me made to order for experiments in fly-
fishing; the water they hold in is good, sometimes very
good, they will take spinners and lures, though somewhat
capriciously, and their condition is at least as good as that
of most of the big kings taken in salt water.

It was shortly after World War II that I decided to
make conscientious efforts to take the Campbell River fish
on a fly. In a sense, plenty of experimenting had been going
on for many years before, as fishermen had been fishing
flies of all kinds over them and near them while searching
for cutthroats and steelhead. So far as I knew, none of these
flies had ever taken a fish, but one or two fish had been
taken on large hair flies trolled for cohos just off the mouth
of the river. This last seemed at least mildly promising, but
I was counting far more on working over the whole range
of Atlantic salmon and steelhead tactics, from deep-sunk
fly to greased line, from small nymphs to the very largest
and brightest of conventional wet flies.

There is no need to go into detail about all this. It is
enough to say that I tried everything I could think of, short
of weighting my flies or putting some kind of spinner
ahead of them, either of which I felt would have destroyed
my purpose. I did try streamer flies, flies dressed on long
Dee hooks, on double hooks and on twisted gut with small
treble hooks behind. I tried bright flies and dull flies, flies
on hooks as small as sixteen and as large as 10/0.

These last were tied for me by my friend Tom Bray-
shaw, in a spirit of co-operation, if not conviction. One day

late in August, Tommy came up to the Islands Pool in the Campbell to supervise my experiments with his big flies. Salmon of thirty, forty, fifty and probably sixty pounds were rolling magnificently all over the pool. I had breast waders and a doublehanded fourteen-foot rod that pushed the big flies well out over the pool. Tommy had chosen to be conservative, with hipwaders, a ten-foot trout rod and smaller flies. We fished for a couple of hours without the slightest effect on the noble fish that continued to roll all about us, though we both agreed that the 10/0 flies looked like good big lures as they came back through the water and certainly should have persuaded any salmon to abandon preconceived notions that a river was no place to feed. My conviction, helped by the big rod and the splendid way the fly settled deep down into the best-lying places, was strong and I worked on towards the tail of the pool. Tommy went back down the bar to where he had left his haversack, fitted a silex casting reel with ninety yards of eighteen-pound monofilament to his trout rod and came back with a two-inch red and silver devon minnow. I decided to stop fishing and watch. At the third cast he had a fish.

At first it seemed quite a co-operative fish—powerful, but willing to leave the fisherman with some illusion that he was controlling the situation. The pool is both long and wide and the bar, running upstream at a long angle, allows one to follow quite nicely. After a moment of hesitation the fish ran for the head and Tommy ran after him, complaining that his situation was desperate and that I was responsible for it. The fish turned back and ran hard and fast for the tail, Tommy with him. Just above the rapids he swirled with considered violence and ran back up again. I offered congratulations and encouragement as Tommy made his way up the bar.

"He's going to stay in the pool," I said. "You'll get him all right."

"With ninety yards of line and an express train on the other end?" said Tommy. "Not bloody likely."

So the fish started down again and Tommy called the result ahead of time, running for all he was worth down the bar. "He's going out of the pool this time. He's got all my line. He's gone." And the fish had gone, down into the bouncing rapid on the far side of the pool. Tommy kept after him, hanging on to the rod. "Now he's got me round a rock in the rapids."

"Can you still feel him?"

"No. He's gone. You feel it." He handed me the rod.

It felt solid and dead. "Have to break, I guess," Tommy said.

"Not from here. You'll lose too much line. Let me wade out into the rapid and see if I can free it."

I believed the fish was gone, but I wasn't wholly convinced, so I recovered line carefuly as I worked my way out into the heavy water. The line remained firm and solid. I got about twenty yards back on to the reel. Then suddenly it was free and tight, shining in the sunlight. There was an explosion of water in the lower pool, seventy yards downstream. The reel gave unhappily under the pressure of my fingers and I started back for shore, the rod held high. Long before I got there the line I had recovered was gone and I was simply holding the fish on the stretch of the nylon. When I got to Tommy the fish was quiet again and I tried to hand him the rod.

"No," he said. "It was all your idea. I've had enough of him."

"You hooked him," I said. "It's your fish and your gear, so you can break in him or lose him, not me."

Tommy took the rod then and we walked down over the rocks to the lower pool, recovering nearly all the line while the fish stayed perfectly quiet.

"What now?" asked Tommy, though he knew as well as I did.

"Stir him up," I said, "before he gets rested."

Tommy shuddered, but he went to work. The fish stirred all right, as though he had been started out of a slingshot, across the pool and down for the tail. In seconds the line was gone and we were running again. The lower pool is quite short, with a long rapid below and fairly deep water along the island side—our side. It was too deep for Tommy's short boots, so I took the rod again while he went round through the island to a gravel bar that showed about half-way down.

The fish was quiet again, well over on the far side, somewhere in the rapids, so I let the line hang slack and paid no attention to him while I waded down. When I was sure I was below him I tightened carefully, thinking the strain might send him up to the pool again. Then I saw him, swimming quite easily to hold station in fast water under the far bank. When I increased the strain he rolled slightly, but made no move to go up. He looked disappointingly small—eighteen or twenty pounds, I judged. I went on down and handed the rod to Tommy.

"I think he's tired," I said. "I can roll him."

"He'd better be," Tommy said. "I'm not going to follow him any farther."

The fish was tired. Tommy worked him carefully across and down the rapid, putting on just enough strain to bring him over and keep him swimming against the current. It was a nice, gentle-handed, skillful performance. When the fish came into the quiet water below the gravel bar he rolled on his side and I tailed him without difficulty, though he was a lot bigger than I had thought—exactly thirty-nine pounds, still silvery and in perfect shape.

Though it was a lot of fun, this was a somewhat discouraging experience and I don't think I ever fished the big flies with real conviction again. For the most part I contented myself with letting my various shapes and sizes and types of flies swing over the big fish when I was looking for steelhead or cutthroats.

Perhaps there is something absurd in this obsession with the fly when it is so abundantly clear that the fish can be taken fairly readily with lures of various types. But under the very limited conditions that offer in the Campbell, where the fish are confined to no more than half a dozen pools in less than two miles of river, any other means than the fly seems pointless. The mere fact that it is difficult, if not impossible, to move these fresh-run fish to the fly raises interesting questions. What protects them? Is it that no fly of any kind reflects anything in their previous experience? Are they restrained by some precise stage of maturity? Or by the bodily processes of adapting from salt to fresh water? Or by the nature of this particular piece of fresh water, its temperature, oxygen values and acidity? Or are their chosen lying places at that particular time unfavorable to the fly? Finally, is there some still untried technique in presenting the fly that will bring a response?

I have complete answers to none of these questions. But since that day when we chased Tommy's fish down the river I have had some experiences that seem worth recording.

One October fourth, several years later, I was looking for a run of cohos that had just come into the river, swinging a No. 4 Silver Brown across a fast, broken, rather deep run. The fly was riding high and a huge, boiling rise intercepted it in midstream. A heavy fish ran with it a short way then stopped, still in the fast water, shaking his head violently. Then he surged in a flurry of white against the current and I could see that he was a very dark fish. Then he broke water completely and there could be no mistake; he was a big black king salmon of forty pounds or more. He threw the fly as he showed himself, but he rolled again immediately, twice more in the same spot, as though he still felt the hook. He was not a fish anybody could possibly have wanted. But he was a big king salmon and he had taken a fairly small orthodox wet fly in fresh water.

On October fourteenth of the following year I was fishing a still smaller Silver Brown from the bar of the Island Pool, again looking for cohos; big kings were breaking all over the pool, a few pink salmon among them. I had a five-ounce rod, a 9/5 leader and lots of line. Near the head of the second main run a big reddish fish took the retrieved fly only a few feet below me. His run was at first rather slow and uneven, but unmistakably powerful. It kept on and on, gradually increasing in speed and liveliness until I was almost convinced I had an unusually large coho. Then he came out on the far side of the pool, about a hundred feet above the break into the rapid, and I knew he was far too big for any coho. I didn't want the fish, but I decided then to try and get my fly back instead of breaking in him. So long as he would keep fighting I felt there was a fair chance.

I had already begun to move upstream from the bar, at the same time working towards my own bank. The fish was still improving his run, slowly, towards the tail of the pool, so I slacked off and paid out line, letting the pull come on him from downstream. He worked up from it nicely, so I tightened again and soon I could see the line cutting water as he swam ponderously past the big rock. I kept moving across the stream and down only a little, to keep a side strain on him, and he began to respond to it, easing across the pool as well as up. I had no real belief that I could keep him in the pool, but I was remembering the big rocks in the rapid that had trapped Tommy's line and I was hoping to bring him to my side of them. The line came in steadily, though never easily, until the backing splice was within a foot or two of the rod top. When he ran again and again I had to slack off to let the drag of the line pull on him from below and keep him from going out of the pool. Twice more I recovered line and he ran off with most of it, but by the second time I had moved down almost to the end of the bar, just above the rapid, and I was able to put on enough side strain to turn him. I recovered line until the current caught him and drew him into the rapid, then I let it tumble him down to the next pool, well inside the big rocks.

When I came up with him, he was holding in the eddy at the head of the lower pool, still upright, still too strong to turn, but not strong enough to swim against the strain I was holding on him. I shortened right up and managed to move in close enough to get a good grip on the wrist of the tail and drag him ashore. The whole performance had taken just over an hour; the fish was reddish bronze, in good condition, quite unmarked, and measured forty-eight inches against my wading staff. It swam off strongly after being freed and held upright in the water for a few seconds.

After this I found it was often not difficult to hook these big fish on small flies once they had moved out into the shallower water. If they chose to go to the bottom and sulk, there was nothing to be done except break the fly off and put on another, but if they chose to fight it was usually possible to beach them and recover the fly after an hour or so of hard work. I never did fish for them deliberately and now I usually avoid using a silver-bodied wet fly at all in those waters after the first week of October. But even so, I once hooked and released two in succession, the first fifty-four inches and the second forty-five inches.

Hooking and playing such large and powerful fish on a light, singlehanded fly rod is interesting and exciting and not without its difficulties. But two factors detract from it: one does not want the fish and so can take any sort of chances without much concern, and one is aware that they have lost the full violence of their power, so the achievement of controlling and beaching them is not really significant. But it does seem significant that they will take a fly at this stage and under these conditions when they will not take it earlier.

That should end the matter tidily for the time being, but it doesn't quite. On September fourteenth about two years ago I was fishing a No. 6 Silver Brown through the Lower Island Pool in the confident expectation of a steelhead. The fly was taken right at the surface, just at the edge of the current and over eight or ten feet of water, by a very large fish. I stumbled at the moment of the take, got my wading staff caught in my jacket and that might well have been the end of it, since I only had an Ox leader; but the fish hesitated briefly after a short run and by the time he went on I had recovered my balance. The run was fast, deep and very strong, down the pool and across, drowning my line in the main current of the pool—I had an eight-foot, four-ounce rod and was making no attempt to check or hold. Apparently he felt the pull of the drowned line, because he swung his run in an arc across the tail of the pool and turned upstream along the far side. Right opposite me he jumped and I saw plainly that he was a king salmon of between thirty and forty pounds, bronze but by no means dark.

Near the head of the pool he turned downstream again and ran back downstream without a pause. I had no intention of following him down the long and awkward rapid, so put on all the strain the rod could reasonably be expected to stand. It had its effect and the next thing I knew he had stopped, about a hundred yards directly downstream from me in a small, secondary pool close under the island. It quickly became obvious he had decided to hold there and sulk. I couldn't go down without letting him out of the pool, so I decided to try walking him upstream. I clamped down on the reel and began to back slowly towards the head of the pool. To my astonishment he came with me, stopping me occasionally and shaking his head

in protest, but making no move to turn and run. I reached
the head of the pool and had just decided it was safe to
recover thirty or forty yards of line and repeat the move
when, it seemed to me, the leader broke. But it hadn't
broken. The fly had pulled out.

This leaves me without any real conclusion at all except
that king salmon will respond to a Silver Brown wet fly
once they have had time to adjust to fresh-water conditions. A somewhat earlier run in a longer river might well
be expected to offer quite exceptional sport to anyone
patient and determined enough to work at it when fish
are showing everywhere and apparently paying no attention. It has also persuaded me that few fish in fresh water
are too much for a four-ounce fly rod and two hundred
yards of backing behind the fly line, even though this is
not the gear I would deliberately choose for king salmon.

7. *The Ocean Years*

Migration is in many stages. First the descent of tiny fry to lake or feeding shallow. Sometime later, the downstream movement of silvering smolts towards the sea, continued through the estuary and the arm or inlet or bay in the relatively low salinity of the surface water. There are the feeding years in the sea itself. Then the slow return, gradually increasing in tempo until the estuary is reached again. And finally the upstream journey, a closely timed race with bodily exhaustion to the redds and the last violent activity of spawning. At each stage the fish is responding to and protected by changes in its body chemistry—it is, in effect, a different creature, suddenly and closely adapted to a new purpose and a new environment.

There are still great downstream movements of salmon. After the big years of the Adams River run, several billion fry move down from the spawning water to Shuswap Lake. A year later tens of millions of these fish, now fingerlings, move down the Thompson and the Fraser to the sea. Two and a half years after that fifteen or twenty million may come back as full-grown fish and between one and two million will be allowed to reach their spawning water and renew the cycle. In the big years of the Chilco and Stuart runs, five or six hundred thousand spawners may send thirty or forty million smolts down to the sea.

But in the smaller streams I watch, the effects of an intense fishery and a closely limited spawning escapement are all too apparent. Twenty-five years ago the cutthroat trout moved upstream in April and one saw them chasing fry even in the middle of the rapids. There is no abundance to bring them now. Twenty-five years ago it was possible to go down to the river's edge in May, scoop out thirty or forty fry in a minute or two and dump them in a Mason jar full of water. For the most part they would be pinks, already silver and on their way to sea, or the slender greenish chums, but often there would be orange-finned cohos and heavily barred, pale-finned king salmon as well. One can watch those same little bays and sheltered places now day after day and never see more than a slim scattering of fry. Even a minnow trap set there will not pick up more than two or three on its best days. Any thought of scooping out a dozen or two to put in a jar and hold up to the sunlight would be sheerest folly—they are not there.

Perhaps the few that are there are enough, but I do not believe they are. Pacific salmon runs should not be a few scattered spawners and a few scattered fry. They are massive and mighty movements, upstream and down, spectacular, wasteful perhaps, but never meager. True, there

is a theoretically ideal spawning abundance, great enough
to use the available gravels, not so great that it leads to loss
through competition for them, and there is no doubt that
it is often attained and occasionally surpassed on the great
commercial rivers where observation and control can be
concentrated. But I wonder if we understand the theoreti-
cal ideal for smaller streams and I wonder still more if
we come near the more complex controls that are necessary to ensure these lesser escapements.

Every stage of migration is critical for the salmons.
Delay in downstream movement of fry and fingerlings can
be almost as damaging as delay in the upstream movement
of spawners. Diversion from normal routes may permit
dangerous concentrations of predators. Unusual water conditions can be enormously destructive. The great Adams
River run of 1958 led to successful spawning by almost
two million fish. The hatch was good; survival and growth
through the year of lake feeding was also good, though
not quite so good as in 1954. As the young fish began
their seaward movement in the spring of 1960 it seemed
reasonable enough to expect a return of ten or twelve
million fish in 1962. But as they passed through the estuary
and reached the sea, the flow of the Fraser was unusually
low, a warning sign that caused the biologists to revise
their estimate sharply downwards. In the end, 1962 brought
back more nearly two million fish than twelve million—
enough to seed the spawning gravels adequately, but with
few if any left over for the commercial catch. This is
serious loss, but not disaster; a single successful cycle
could restore the immense abundance of 1958, when nearly
twenty million fish were taken in the commercial catch.

But it is highly suggestive of the need for a full complement of spawners on the beds of every river in every year if the fish are to maintain themselves in the face of natural uncertainties.

Until about ten years ago, not much was precisely known about the ocean movements of the salmon. It was known that a certain number of fish undertook only a limited migration, in some instances living out their sea lives in the larger, partially enclosed bodies of water such as Puget Sound and the Gulf of Georgia. The great majority moved northwestward along the coast line, fish from Oregon and Washington moving far up into waters of British Columbia, British Columbia fish carrying through into Alaskan waters. At least some Alaskan fish moved southward, through the passes between the Aleutian Islands. But it was generally assumed that most of the migrants found their feed and lived their lives more or less within the hundred-fathom line of the continental shelf—not more than thirty or forty miles offshore.

The North American salmon fishery has always been limited to territorial waters. This is logical, because the salmon must return to their rivers, they are at maximum size and peak condition as they do so and they are well concentrated. It is much easier to control such a fishery to ensure proper spawning escapements and individual runs can be identified and protected with some accuracy.

Asian stocks of Pacific salmon, originating principally in Russian waters, are even larger than North American stocks and include all the same species. The Japanese have long conducted an intensive fishery for these stocks and first developed a high-seas fishery which extended well

over towards North American waters in the 1930's. This
fishery ceased in 1938 on protest from the United States
that North American runs were being affected. It was
not resumed again intensively until 1954. In the meanwhile
Japan had signed, with Canada and the United States, the
North Pacific Fisheries Treaty which specified, among
other things, that the signing nations would abstain from
fishing stocks that were being fully used by the other
nations involved. It also set a provisional dividing line
between east and west at 175° West Longitude.

It was obvious from the start that this line might mean
much or little, since no one knew how far North American salmon travel westward across the Pacific, how far
east the Asian salmon travel or how much the two stocks
intermingle. In the years since 1954 the three treaty nations
have carried on ambitious and sophisticated research to
answer these questions.

The investigation, which still continues, is costing about
two million dollars a year and employs fifteen or sixteen
large research vessels. It has involved the tagging of tens
of thousands of salmon, caught mainly by purse seiner and
surface long-lines. It has led to the development of special
techniques for distinguishing between salmon of the same
species from different localities—blood counts, identification of parasites, close examination of scales, measurements
and counts of fin rays, vertebrae and other physical characteristics have all proved of value in distinguishing between
Asiatic and North American fish, and even between fish
from different parts of the same continent.

The work is still far from complete, but it is abundantly
clear that fish from Alaska in the east and Kamchatka in

the west do meet and intermingle in important numbers over some two thousand miles of the North Pacific Ocean. Though the northwestward movement of southern fish along the North American coast line through the Aleutians and into Bristol Bay has been amply confirmed, it is also true that large numbers of Alaskan fish move westward into the Bering Sea during the summer and then are forced southward through the Aleutians by the cold of winter. A similar eastward movement of Kamchatka fish is forced down to a wintering area below the Aleutians and extending as far southward as 40°N Latitude. Sockeye salmon from Bristol Bay travel westward as far as 170°E. Longitude, Alaska chums as far as 172°E. Asian stocks of pinks and chums, which have been estimated as two or three times greater than North American stocks, are known to travel as far eastward as 150°W Longitude.

In a general way the provisional line of 175°W has proved accurate enough. Asian stocks predominate to the east of it, Alaskan stocks to the west; Canadian and Pacific Northwest stocks do not seem to reach the line in significant numbers. If both Alaskan and Japanese fishermen were fishing in the same way and were ensuring and caring for roughly equal spawning escapements in their own streams, the provisional line would probably serve quite well. But North American fishermen are not allowed to fish for salmon on the high seas, so they cannot possibly take any Asian fish, while the Japanese, having accepted the fact that North American stocks are fully used and so qualify under the abstention principle, should only be taking Asian fish. Since American stocks persist in some numbers at least as far as 175°E, and since they are indiscriminately mingled with Asian fish, Japanese fishermen are certainly taking them in inconsiderable numbers. So Alaskans can properly argue that they are protecting fish from their own fishermen so that Japanese can take them. At the same time the Japanese can point out that since bad weather limits North Pacific high seas fishing to very short seasons and since large numbers of Asian fish travel east of the provisional line, they are being prevented from taking a full harvest of Asian fish.

Under international law the Japanese position is a strong one. The high seas are open to all nations and no other nation has shown such skill and ingenuity in developing high seas fisheries; no other nation has greater need of the yield of its fisheries. Japanese acceptance of the abstention principle and the provisional line are important concessions.

Against this, it is readily demonstrable that high-seas fishery for salmon makes little or no sense except in the case of nations like Japan, which have only limited salmon stocks of their own. Salmon are very easily caught by commercial methods and they are most easily caught as they approach their home rivers, when they are at maximum size and in ideal condition. Japanese proponents of the high-seas fishery argue that a larger total harvest can be realized by catching immature fish in the ocean because losses to predators and other natural causes are heavy enough to exceed increase by growth between this stage and the return to territorial waters; but the balance of evidence is against this. It seems rather that the final stages of growth are rapid enough to exceed normal losses by a considerable margin.

In addition to its other disadvantages, a high-seas fishery

for salmon is extremely difficult, if not impossible, to control with any accuracy, since it takes fish of inseparably intermixed stocks and at varying stages of maturity. No doubt controls of some sort could be developed in time, but both development and enforcement would be difficult and extremely costly, and it is inconceivable that they could approach the accuracy of controls applied in territorial waters.

All these seem to me powerful arguments against any high-seas fishery for salmon. But there is a final argument that makes a high-seas fishery an absurdity. In the face of advancing industrial civilization, the essential fresh-water habitat of the salmon can be preserved only by the most conscientious care, and then only at some economic cost to other uses of water. It is highly unlikely that any nation will give such care and face such costs for fish that are to be caught on the high seas by another nation. Some form of agreement might be made between the nations concerned, on a temporary basis; but in the end the rivers would be sacrificed to other purposes and the salmon would disappear.

One may have every sympathy for the Japanese need of protein food and the warmest admiration for their skill and knowledge as fishermen, but it is impossible not to be concerned about this ultimate prospect. It has already proved difficult enough to preserve salmon runs for our own fishermen, and some have been lost to industrial development; in many ways it is reasonable to hope that we shall do better than we have in the past. But it is against human nature to suppose that public sympathy for the salmon runs could be maintained as it should be if signifi-

cant numbers of the fish are being taken by other nations
that do not share in the effort of protection.

There is a great deal of research still to be done by the
North Pacific Fisheries Commission and it is not unreasonable to hope that equitable, logical and scientifically clear
solutions to international problems will come from it. It
is a great advance to know that salmon do travel to mid-
ocean and beyond, mingle with stocks from another continent, yet still separate themselves in due time and return
faithfully to their home streams. It is important to learn
more about the relationship of losses to growth at various
stages of maturity. Above all, it is important to know more
about the "sea disasters" that can now only be inferred
from the fact that large and apparently successful migra-
tions of smolts sometimes bring disproportionately small
returns of adult fish. Submarine earthquakes and volcanic
disturbances, shifts of current and changes of temperature
are among the probable causes, and presumably little could
be done to counteract them. But some advance knowledge
of the nature and size of the damage would be of value
to the fishery itself and would also permit proper management of the depleted run.

I should admit, perhaps, that my own interest is somewhat less practical. I should like to know the exact movements of fish from various rivers, the currents that influence them, the types and concentrations of ocean feed that
sustain and develop them. I should like to know how and
why an Asian fish decides to turn westward and a North
American fish eastward from the same mid-ocean feeding
area. Hereditary response to the position of the sun? It
seems a good answer, but if all the Pacific salmons first

developed into their species in the Sea of Japan and the Sea of Okhotsk, how did the North American fish learn their navigation? In my own lifetime, many questions about salmon have been answered, many mysteries have been revealed. But every answer, every revelation serves only to make those graceful forms lying over the gravel at the headwaters of a mountain stream a more affecting miracle.

8. *The Energy of Salmon*

ANGLERS HAVE A DIRECT INTEREST IN the energy of fish and we talk about it all the time, usually in terms of how strongly and violently our fish react when hooked. It is generally conceded that we exaggerate grossly and make gentle and inoffensive creatures sound like wounded buffaloes and man-eating tigers. But this is one of our cherished conventions. It grows out of the inadequate way we arm ourselves, the difficulties we accept or create for ourselves and the high significance we manage to assign to our successes and failures.

There is relativity even in exaggeration and our highly subjective observations have established a few conclusions that stand up to closer examination. Those of us who fish for anadromous fish, for instance, know that fish fresh in from salt water nearly always fight faster and harder, though not necessarily longer, than fish that have been in fresh water for some time. Sexually immature fish are usually more active than fish approaching maturity or those that have previously spawned. Small fish are likely to be more active than larger fish of the same species and possibly stronger for their size, even though their effects are less impressive. It is an illusion, or at best a partial truth, that fish fight harder in very cold water. The salmon and trout, for instance, are extremely active in cold summer temperatures—water that is between forty-five and fifty-five degrees Fahrenheit—but they are noticeably less active in water temperatures below forty degrees Fahrenheit. Fish in peak summer or fall condition perform better than in early spring.

Even these fairly broad conclusions have always been open to some question, because individual fish vary somewhat, the type of gear on which they are caught varies considerably and the conditions under which they are caught may vary enormously. But the energy of fish, especially migratory fish, has now become a matter of considerable economic importance; it is important to know, for instance, how fast an upstream migrant can be expected to travel through a fishway over a high dam or how much effort a downstream migrant can be expected to exert against the pull of a turbine intake. Tagging of migrant fish raises the question of how many can be expected to die through the stress of capture and handling. Industrial pollutions and increased temperatures through industrial activities raise similar questions. As a result, much valuable scientific work has been done in the past ten years. A good deal of it has direct application to the questions anglers commonly ask themselves and all of it sheds interesting light on how and why fish perform as they do.

It has been known for some while that the recovery of salmon caught and marked in the ocean has been disproportionately low. Recoveries of troll-caught king and coho salmon, for instance, have been as low as twenty per cent in a fishery known to be taking over eighty-five per cent of the total runs. Even when allowance is made for natural mortality, the gap is much too large and suggests some serious injury to the fish in the process of tagging or capture or both.

Fish caught at sea by commercial trolling vessels are subjected to considerable stress—they strike at a large lure drawn through the water by a steel line carrying a fifty-pound weight. The vessel itself continues on its way at normal trolling speed and in due time the line is recovered on a power-driven spool and the fish is brought to boat. It must then be handled, tagged and released.

As a check on the effects of all this, numbers of king and coho salmon were caught and tagged in the usual way and then held in live boxes under conditions considered as nearly as possible ideal for recovery. In various experiments mortality varied from twenty to seventy per cent and was invariably associated with a very high concentration of lactic acid in the blood stream—a level in excess of 125 milligrams per cent, compared to normal levels of about fifteen milligrams per cent. This high level was reached only gradually and most fish died two or three hours after capture. After six hours there were very few deaths and blood samples had begun to show recovery.

These experiments are of great interest to the sportsman because they suggest that the hard fighting fish he generously releases, apparently in good condition, may have only a very limited chance of surviving. They become of even greater interest when compared with similar experiments on salmon in fresh water. It was found that salmon could not be made to struggle as violently against restraint as they would in salt water and they were much quieter while being handled and tagged. Even though they were forced to swim until exhausted, the lactic-acid concentrations in the blood did not rise above seventy-five milligrams per cent, and none of the fish died.

It is fairly obvious that these differences reflect the different demands on the fish in fresh and salt water. Salt-water life demands intermittent but violent activity—swift pursuit of smaller creatures in feeding, prompt and explosive violence in flight from predators. Flight from the attack of seal or shark must be instantaneous and, since the issue is death or survival, muscles respond to their extreme limit. Within seconds the issue is decided; the fish is dead or else free to rest and recover from its momentary explosion of activity. The danger of hook and line is different, but the muscular response is the same—immediate and violent effort to escape. Usually there is no escape, but the effort persists, even after the line is recovered and the fish is lifted into the boat. In most cases the demand has been too great, energy has been driven beyond the point of recovery and the fish dies.

The demands of fresh-water life are altogether different. There is no feeding; predators are few and inefficient. The fish draws on body reserves of oil and fat and must make its way with paced endurance against the rapids and falls and turbulence of a swift-flowing river to its hereditary spawning grounds. The stimulus is the current itself, per-

sistent, varying only in its strength. The response is calculated to meet it, perhaps a period of steady swimming
against moderate flow, perhaps a brief and powerful effort
against a vicious rapid. In either case there will be rest
before exhaustion, a refusal of the body to struggle further
without time for recovery.

The precise physiology that controls this change and
protects the fish from reactions that would promptly kill
him in the new environment is obscure, but there is no
doubt that glands, the pituitary especially, play a large
part. The effects are of profound interest to every angler
who fishes for anadromous fish. They fully confirm the
long-held conviction that fresh-run fish fight much harder
and more violently than fish that have been in from the
sea for several days, and at the same time give warning
that the release of a fresh fish that has fought exceptionally
hard must be undertaken with extreme care. They explain
the so-called sulking of a heavy fish that works down to
the bottom and will not move; he has reached the point
of exhaustion beyond which he will not exert himself and
seeks protection in hiding rather than flight. It may well
be that a fish hooked on light gear and handled rather
gently will be less likely to sulk than one hooked on heavy
gear and forced to violent response; and perhaps the best
way to cure a sulking fish is to allow him his rest with the
least possible disturbance, then gradually apply pressure
from a new direction.

It seems clear that a feeding fish in salt water is rather
a poor risk for release, but even here the angler has important advantages. His tackle is lighter and probably does
not subject the fish to such extremes of stress as does com-

mercial trolling gear. Release is usually possible without lifting the fish from the water, especially if a single hook is used, so there is none of the stress that handling and tagging entail. Fish undoubtedly become better and better risks as they approach their rivers and reduce their feeding rate with the onset of maturity. Any fish that is holding off the mouth of the home river and feeding little or not at all, as is usually the case with large king salmon, is very unlikely to drive himself beyond the point of recovery. Any dark fish and any fish that has entered its river can be released with full certainty of recovery provided it is not injured in some other way, though it is just possible that a few absolutely fresh-run cohos, steelheads and Atlantic salmon that have entered their streams well before spawning time may drive themselves beyond the point of recovery.

There remains the question of feeding fish that normally live their whole lives in fresh water. Dr. E. C. Black, of the University of British Columbia, who conducted most of the experiments I have outlined above, has similarly tested one- and two-year-old Kamloops trout. Kamloops trout are at least as violently active when hooked as any fresh-water fish I know. Dr. Black found that the fish, especially the yearlings, could be driven to the point where the lactic-acid concentrations passed the salmon's danger level of 125 milligram per cent, but that recovery was comparatively rapid and during four years of experiment no fish died of these effects. It is clear from this that fresh-water fish can be released without fear of death from exhaustion, though they must always be handled with reasonable care to prevent other types of injury.

Nothing in all this is really new to the experienced and well-read fisherman, but it is satisfying to find proper biological confirmation for ideas and convictions until now largely empirical. Even now, the precise mechanics of exhaustion to death are not fully understood, as Dr. Black is careful to explain. The high levels of lactic acid in the blood are not necessarily the cause of death, though they coincide with death. It is known that a disturbance of this magnitude reduces the power of the blood to combine with oxygen and carbon dioxide and the capacity of the heart to pump blood. The really significant point is that the build-up of the concentration continues in fish over a period of several hours after violent exercise, while in mammals it ceases with the activity and recovery begins immediately. So a fish that is released promptly, in apparently excellent condition, almost certainly has not yet reached the full state of exhaustion brought on by his struggles.

By interpreting the energy of fish in terms of practical interest to anglers, 1 do not want to discount the importance of energy studies in the protection and management of salmon. The Pacific salmon enters his river as a precise machine, carrying with him enough reserves of fat and protein to allow him to make his upstream journey, develop to full maturity, dig the nest and complete the spawning act; there will be little or nothing left over. These energy reserves he carries with him are hereditary and so exact that a delay of three days will impair spawning efficiency and delays of twelve days will prevent spawning entirely. In other words, a salmon must find his river in much the same state as his ancestors found it or his race will die out.

High dams and other severe obstructions are common and destructive causes of delay and they may lead to serious waste of energy as fish struggle against the turbulence of the tailrace or fight their way through a long and steep by-pass. But there are other, less obvious, man-made demands on energy that can be as damaging as delay at an obstruction. A fish may be successful in passing through a stretch of polluted river, but the decreased oxygen content of the water will have forced him to work harder and reduce his total strength. Any significant change in a river's temperature, and such changes can be caused by industrial wastes and cooling, by storage dams or by atomic power plants, will make demands on the fish's slim store of energy. Any change in the physical and chemical values of water, such as may be brought about by a large storage lake behind a high dam, is likely to cause confusion and delay in migrating fish—and so waste energy.

These are subtle effects. They may not, in themselves, kill immediately and visibly. But each one draws upon the precisely limited reserves of energy in the body of the fish. It may, by itself, be a great enough demand to prevent successful spawning or it may be only one of several unnatural demands that together exhaust the fish before its time. All such things are abuses of river systems that can and should be controlled or prevented. But proper control is only possible if the precise nature and degree of the effects is fully understood. The main purpose of energy studies is to achieve this measure of understanding, but there is a fine, sharp pleasure also in merely knowing a little more of the perfect precision that is built into the body of a returning salmon.

9. *The Death of the Salmon*

D<small>O THEY ALL DIE AFTER SPAWNING? YES.</small>
Even the pink salmon after a life of less than two years?
Even the great and powerful king salmon? Even the jacks,
the precocious males that come back after only one short
year in the sea? Yes, they all die. Not a single one of all
the hosts upon hosts that come in from the sea lives to
spawn a second time.

It is natural for a man to resent this, I suppose, to feel
that it is wasteful and shocking, in some way unnatural.
Many years ago, when I first came to the rivers of the
Pacific salmon, I refused to believe it. After all, some steelhead and Atlantic salmon live to spawn a second time,
even a third and fourth and fifth time. One sees them,
bright and clean and strong again, in the rivers after spawning and knows that the power of recovery is in them. For
years I searched among Pacific salmon for some sign of
recovery, for even one fish that seemed to have renewed

its grip on life. I did not find it. I have seen chum salmon
back in salt water but invariably they were pathetic, worn-
out creatures still in the immediate process of dying. Now
I have lived so long with this fact of collective, simultaneous
death that I no longer resent or question it. Instead I find
it fitting and beautiful, certainly useful in some way or
ways that are not entirely clear and a yearly occasion of
high drama. I am still curious about the manner and meaning of it, but I do not question that it has manner and
meaning.

In many ways the short-run rivers are best for watching
the spawning salmon. When fish have run several miles
upriver from the sea, one expects them to be battered and
scarred and weary. But in the short-run rivers it is clear
that any changes are in them and of them. One sees everything, from the first arrivals, through all the modifications
of color and habit and performance, to the very end.

The actual arrival of a big run of salmon is a surprisingly
subtle thing, in spite of the size of the fish and the mass
of the schools. One can live right beside the mouth of a
stream and hardly know that run has turned into it. I have
sat in an anchored boat at the mouth of the Nimpkish
River and watched school after school of cohos turn in
through a whole afternoon and evening. The schools were
big, sometimes hundreds of fish closely packed and only
a few feet under the surface. Sometimes their passage
showed in faint ripples on the surface, more rarely in swirls
as they turned in some sudden panic. Sometimes a school
turned downstream, turned again and came back. I do not
remember that a single fish jumped in the river channel,
though there were occasional jumpers to the north, just

before the schools turned in. For the most part I was watching only a narrow strip of water, perhaps a hundred feet wide, between the boat and the north edge of the channel; how many thousands of fish passed around me and behind me, I have no idea. But at the end of it all there was an odd sense of disbelief in the whole affair. There was little or no sign of fish on the rising tide upstream; there was only the visual memory of those hundreds of bright clean bodies, timid yet purposeful, slipping secretly into the river that had spawned them. Had there really been so many?

The Campbell is a broad, shallow stream where it passes my house. Thousands of salmon and steelhead run up through that stretch every year, yet I have scarcely ever seen one on its way. The large movements may well be at night and in daylight it would be natural enough for fish to pass stealthily through such an open, shallow reach, but it is still a surprise to find them suddenly in the pools farther upstream, a few hundred pink salmon towards the end of July, the big king salmon by the first week of August. Over the deep strong water of the pools they are not afraid to show themselves, the pinks breaking the surface like rising trout, the kings rolling out and shouldering over with a power that breaks the water white and starts echoes from the banks.

At this stage there is nothing confiding about the fish. They have their full strength; they are not ripe for spawning and they are keyed to protect themselves from whatever dangers may threaten. The silvery brightness of salt water is gone, but change towards spawning shape and color is gradual, almost imperceptible at first in these early fish. One fishes a fly over them and among them in search of steelhead, cutthroat or early-running coho, grateful for the magnificent way they show themselves, occasionally casting to cover one that is rolling persistently in the same place. Nothing comes of it except the rare, breathtaking coincidence of rolling side and drifting fly. But who is to say that nothing more than this is possible?

Later, with the cold, wet winds of early November, all this is changed. The fish are in the shallows now, active all across them. The gravel is loosened, freshly gray and brown where it has been turned by the tails of the females. Most of the pink salmon have spawned and died but kings and chums are everywhere, spawning, dying and dead. There are a few cohos among them and even one or two scarlet-bodied, green-headed creek sockeyes.

At such times I usually leave my rod on the bank and wade slowly upstream among the fish, pausing long and often to lean on my wading staff and watch. So long as I am slow and careful they do not rush away from me. It is easy to approach within reach of man's many tools of destruction, a little less so to approach within reach of the less deadly claws and teeth that are a bear's tools; from this threat they will rush a few yards upstream, throwing spray with their great broad tails. It is time then to stand still.

Any real concern for self-preservation has largely left them. They are obsessed with sexual purpose and the imminence of death leaves no leeway for other concerns. A month ago they would have started, arrow-swift, from a shadow. A month ago these shallows that they cling to with such urgency would have seemed places of terror to them. A month ago there was neither male nor female in their concerns. The new preoccupation is physical and mechanical, of course, but it is also ruthlessly logical even in its disregard for the dangers that may defeat it, because the time for fulfillment is so short. Successful spawning is the preservation of the race; within a month, spawned or unspawned, these strong bodies will be little more than a few scattered vertebrae and horny gill covers.

As I stand still in the hurrying water they settle back to their fierce pursuits and plungings, to gentle, questing swimming, to holding and swaying and shifting. Here and there a female shows her broad side in the fierce, flat thrust of nest digging. Great fish brush against my waders, even pass calmly between my legs. I am nothing to them unless an odd-shaped tree root caught on the shallows. Watching their eyes that neither see nor meet with mine, my mood tells me that they know me, know my concern for them and are not afraid. I do not have time then—nor want it— to remember that a bear waiting quietly to scoop them to death would find the same acceptance until he moved. A bear has his part there, inherited from his ancestors; but then I, too, am a rightful spectator, my way paid by under-standing, my part to watch, to sympathize, to enjoy, to hope that there will never be less of them on these fall shallows than I count today.

Shallows like these are not the best place to watch spawn-ing; the surface of the water is too much broken by its speed over the rocky gravels and light strikes from it in all directions, distorting shapes and colors, obscuring the detail of movement. Yet there is much to be seen. The king salmon females are usually rusty red, their males almost black. The bodies of both have lost much of their heavy-shouldered thickness; often they are scarred and blotched with destroying fungus. Male and female are by no means always easy to separate, except by their actions; a female coho may be as black of head, as crimson of body, with jaws almost as heavily hooked as her mate, but it is she that will dig the nest, not he. The pink salmon males are fantastically humped, most of them now dying, while the females hold a certain grace of shape in spite of their exhaustion.

Generally I move slowly upstream to a prow-shaped maple whose mossy trunk reaches horizontally ten or fifteen feet over the water before rearing up towards its crown. It is a good place to watch when the light is right. The water is too easy and shallow for the big kings, but chum salmon spawn directly under the tree and for fifty or a hundred feet upstream. Once I watched a small and lively female at work there, shadowed by five large males. The vivid black stripe of her side, edged with gold, showed clearly as she turned to stir the gravel. Then the males closed over her in a struggling mass and she forced from among them to break the surface and show that black and golden side in the air. The whole thing was repeated several times and I never did see the end of it or understand its real pattern and purpose. I have seen the shudder of spending fish close under the crooked maple, the lifting of their heads, the opening of their jaws, the clouding of milt in the bottom of the egg pocket. But in watching from above one can never see all the intricacies of the spawning act or understand fully the closely interdependent parts of male and female.

In the little streams one can see everything much more

clearly, but the fish are less confiding—one must keep one's distance or they will start away and scatter. Even so, their colors are plain and the patterns of movement seem less haphazard and confusing. Occasionally, when two fish are paired apart from the others, it is possible to recognize the significant intricacies of behavior that are fully revealed only in the observation tank.

Throughout the nest digging of the female, it is the male's part to stimulate her. He does this by continuously and closely circling over her so that his belly lightly touches her back. If his circling becomes too high, he expels one or two air bubbles from his swim bladder and sinks deeper; if he finds himself bearing too heavily upon her he rises to the surface, takes in more air and resumes his circling at the proper depth. From time to time, usually when she settles back into the gravel hollow to test its depth with her anal fin, he settles beside her, vibrating his body against hers, raising his head, opening his jaws, occasionally even shedding an involuntary jet of milt. Unless the female has decided the nest is ready, all this is without effect and she thrusts violently forward again on her side, throwing gravel back with her tail. When all is ready the two hold side to side, their vents closely over the depression in the gravel. Their bodies shudder powerfully, heads rise together, jaws open wide, curving bodies force deeply down into the egg pocket as eggs and milt are shed together. The whole process is repeated several times before the fish are finally spent and ready for death.

This death is no anticlimax, nor is it the inevitable consequence of spawning. Precocious male Pacific salmon that have never been to salt water, like their Atlantic counterparts, spawn successfully and do not die. It is not simply a matter of old age; Dr. O. H. Robertson of California has kept castrated sockeye salmon alive and healthy for seven and eight years, or about twice their normal life span. Yet it is a particularly complete and, in a sense, perfect death because everything about the fish—blood, tissues, organs, the whole body in all its parts—ages simultaneously. The salmon dies, not as man does, through the failure of some single part of him while the rest is healthy; he dies totally, his whole life force used up in the fulfillment of return and reproduction.

Dr. Robertson has shown that this is brought about chiefly by the extraordinary activity of the pituitary and adrenal glands that accompanies—and presumably in large measure controls—the maturing and spawning of a full-grown Pacific salmon. In other words the salmon's life is a gradual crescendo from the moment he turns towards his river and the violent activity of the spawning beds.

Even in the short-run rivers a few salmon die without spawning; if they are held away from the shallows by heavy floods, many may pass their time and die unspent. But under normal conditions there is a safety factor of several days between the covering of the last eggs in the final nest and death. Once I pitied the salmon in this state. Now I love them. They are death itself in a shell of life, but that remaining shell of life, though without hope or reason beyond the safety factor it provides, is impressive. The fish conserve strength by sheltering in the bays and eddies of rivers and in the quieter water near the banks. Raccoons and bears find them easily there, the predatory sea gulls dive down at them until at last there is no longer strength to support them even in the lessened currents; they turn sideways, lose balance, drift and die.

But until that last strength is gone the will to live is still in them and finds its expression. At some too close threat of danger they will still drive away, upstream or down, in a surge of energy that seems no proper part of their wasted shapes. Bodies white with parasitic fungus, great king salmon somehow hold station over swift-running spawning shallows as though they still could play a part. I see them now on the shallows near my house, often two fish together, slowly forced down by the current, turning fiercely against it as it presses on their broad thin flanks and warns them of their weakness. It is the sort of thing man has glorified in himself as the undying spirit of man. Seeing it here so clearly, long after hope and purpose have gone, I can recognize it for what it is: the undying spirit of animals. I find it no less admirable.

PART THREE
Estuary Fishing

1. *The Nature of Estuaries*

I REMEMBER THINKING, AS A VERY SMALL boy, that one of the supreme sights of the world must be the mouth of a river. I could not satisfactorily imagine this meeting of the river's flow and the sea's surge and I knew it would be a waste of time to ask anyone to describe it to me. Just what I expected I am not at all sure, but I suppose some sudden and violent outpouring of fresh water into salt, plainly visible, dramatic and splendid. I knew little or nothing of tides and even less of the fearful things men do to river mouths in the process of civilization. So the first few estuaries I did finally see were disappointing and unconvincing.

Since that time I have seen many river mouths, large and small, and known many estuaries, spoiled and unspoiled. In general it is true that river mouths are not spectacular; one has to know and understand something of them to appreciate them. Even the youngest and wildest rivers tend to cushion their approach to immolation by building deltas of gravel and sand and mud. They slow down, wander into many channels, sharing these with the ebb and flow of the tides, and so meet the sea only in gradual transformation. It is interesting to remember that Captain George Vancouver, who made the first really thorough exploration of the Pacific Coast from California northward, failed to discover the mouths of the two largest rivers he passed, the Columbia and the Fraser. The Columbia, meeting the ocean majestically, disguises itself in the crashing white breakers that form and reform over its massive sand bars. The Fraser hides in a dozen channels through mud and sand flats; Vancouver thought them navigable only by canoes. Farther up the coast he was disappointed again and again at the heads of the long inlets to find that they ended in "swampy low land" among the high mountains. Later, the first settlers built their homes near these low and swampy places, raised cattle on the slough hay and salt grasses and bred families of children who remembered the secrets of the tide flats all their lives.

This, then, is likely to be the way of estuaries. Only when one has walked the flat places and heard the wind in the grasses, explored the sloughs and side channels, watched the tides and faced the storms, does a river mouth take on character and substance and reveal its dramatic power. I know a few smaller streams that enter the sea directly, over falls or through rock-walled canyons, but even these are likely to have their flats of sand or gravel, revealed by the ebb of a long run-out, that time and flow will one day build higher.

Any estuary can be fished and most have fish somewhere

about them—of all the angler's "likely places," few are more likely than where fresh and salt water meet and mingle. But the mouths of very large rivers are much like the sea itself; the river is lost in them and the fisherman becomes lost in them—he is fishing not an estuary but some little part of a great confusing reach of water. Even rivers of moderate size become very large where they meet the tides; too often one needs a boat and some very special local knowledge which leads to sloughs and side channels. Sometimes the main channel is exposed in pools and runs and riffles at low tide and there is nothing much better than this. But my preference is for the small streams and the creeks that one can manage—though often with difficulty—from one's feet and whose form and pattern is rarely altogether lost.

The sea trout of the Pacific Coast is the cutthroat. The rainbow runs to sea and becomes the steelhead, but he rarely lingers long in estuary waters. The Dolly Varden is also a sea-running fish, and in some estuaries he is fairly abundant, but he is not the equal of the cutthroat either as a fish or a fly-fisherman's fish. Cutthroats often run in good numbers to tiny creeks and may be found off them at certain tides and times. But the best cutthroat creeks are usually of fair size and, for some reason as yet unexplained, often have the amber-colored water of the cedar swamps rather than clear flow of the mountains.

In this day of detailed research, surprisingly little is known of the cutthroat, especially in his sea-running phase. Life history, migration stages, feeding habits, stream preferences, all are matters of vague surmise and angler's observation. Even his peak spawning time remains a matter for debate, although it probably varies a good deal from one watershed to another. I know of no significant tagging program that has been carried out with migratory cutthroat, and I have only recently heard of a serious effort towards accurate scale reading.

In my experience, sea-running cutthroats rarely exceed four pounds, which suggests that they have a considerably more restricted migration than steelhead or salmon. They seem to spawn for the first time at fourteen or fifteen inches in length and a weight of about one and a half pounds; larger fish may be spawning for a second or third time. These larger fish seem to enter the rivers in July and August, well ahead of the main spawning run which comes in about the middle of November and is accompanied by good numbers of fish of about the same size that are not going to spawn. Spawning starts some time after Christmas and lasts until March, with a February peak in most streams. But there can be significant variations in both the timing and character of all these movements.

It is possible that cutthroats wander a considerable distance in salt water from their home rivers and they may enter other estuaries or streams to feed—there is nothing really to prove or disprove these theories, though precise knowledge would be important in management. But it is quite clear that some cutthroats are to be found in the estuaries of all but the smallest creeks in every month of the year. This is what makes them the main factor in estuary fishing; one may find other fish, but the cutthroats make it worthwhile to go fishing in the first place.

Tides play a big part in estuary fishing, but I must admit that after all these years I am never quite sure what it is.

Fish do move in and upstream with the flood tide and they often feed well as they move. But they also feed well as they move downstream on the ebb. Both feeding and movement are generally better on large tides than on small ones, and I am quite sure that I have caught more estuary fish on the last two hours of a long ebb and the first hour of the flood than at any other stage. But I have also fished these stages a great deal more.

Estuaries, even of streams that are approximately the same size, differ enormously, and I think that common sense and personal preference, as well as those two fallibles, experience and local knowledge, should be allowed to enter into the choice of a fishing tide. Most of the small-stream estuaries I know fall into three main types. There are those which run out over shallow gravel bars, often dividing into several small channels; those which enter cleanly at high tide over a fall or a rocky bed and cut a long channel through sand or mud flats covered by salt water except on the lowest tides; and those that enter through salt-water meadows, cutting a long channel between high mudbanks. The first type is the most difficult and I suspect the least productive; the fish are usually scattered and one can only wade out hopefully with the last of the ebb and retreat gradually before the flood. At times, especially on the spring-fry run, the fish concentrate in the main channel as the flood comes well up in it, but one is usually backed into the brush by then and too close to them.

The second type is my favorite and is obviously most interesting to fish on a long ebb, when the flats are bare and the stream's channel across them is approachable and clearly defined. Such channels are often deeply cut and hold fish at all stages of tide, though it is logical to work out with the tide. On really low tides one can move right to the end of the channel and find fish feeding along the edge of the drop-off beyond it, then follow the tide back again as the flood starts up the channel. These streams usually have one or two well-defined tidal pools that can make sudden spells of good fishing towards the peak of the flood. But they are often disappointing and I rarely wait for that stage of the flood if I have found fish on the low tide.

The third type of estuary, where the stream has cut its channel through tidal meadows, is in many ways the most delightful of all. The low flatland gives a strong sense of space and freedom; every breeze over it is full of sound and meaning, changing the greens of weeds and grass in springtime, rattling the seed pods and dry stems of summer and fall. Mallard and pintails jump from sloughs and potholes, Wilson snipe flash from the grass knots and plunge down again into new hiding places; fall may bring a flock of snow geese or white fronts in migration. There is always life and movement somewhere on the flats and it has about it a special quality of wildness that belongs with salt spray and sea storms.

Where a river of fair size makes its way across such flats it is logical to fish the last of the ebb and the first of the flood. The main channel takes on the shape and character of its river; then one can move freely and the fish are more easily found. Often there are deepwater pools under the cut banks where some fish hold regardless of the retreating tide. There are riffles and runs and eddies. and plenty of current to help put life into the fly. But in the smaller

streams none of this holds. When the channel is emptied
of tide the stream's flow is too slight and shallow to hold
fish. The few that are left behind are nervous and rarely
feeding—one sees them by the ripple of their movement
and knows the movement for flight or panic search for
shelter. Intermediate tides are often favorable in these estuaries, though the last of the flood and the start of the ebb
on big tides are likely to be most productive.

There is also a fourth type of stream to consider, so small
that it has no real estuary at all and no clearly marked
channel beyond its mouth. Many such streams breed considerable runs of both coho salmon and cutthroat trout,
even though they may be so small that one can step across
them in summer. As streams they are unfishable; one can
poke a worm or a fly through the bush into some likely
spot and perhaps hook a good fish but, profitable and demanding though this may be, interest in it tends to fade
after one is ten or twelve years old and has learned to cast.
The only real possibility is to meet the fish as they come
to the creek's slight influence on a full-flood tide or find
them as they hold and feed near the drop-off from its beach.

Either venture can be surprisingly successful when conditions are right. Finding the feeding fish at the drop-off is
the less likely of the two and more demanding of precise
local knowledge, but it yields a fine sense of achievement
and very lively fishing. In the fall, usually in late September or October, both cohos and cutthroats will be holding
off the creek, waiting for the rains to bring it up and let
them in. Sometimes they take freely and well, more often
they are scattered and uncertain, especially for the fly-
fisherman. But they are always worth a fly-fisherman's

attention. Whether he can catch them or not, fish will be showing. He may grow weary with casting and curse the choice that limits his distance to fifty or sixty feet where the spinner is getting a hundred and fifty, but the very next cast and retrieve may get him a three-pound cutthroat or an old cock coho of ten or fifteen pounds. If he reflects for a moment he will remember that he has spent many weary hours on lakes far less attractive than his chosen creek mouth and without the slightest chance of such solid rewards as these.

These, then, are my estuaries, little places, often unconsidered, highly uncertain, pleasantly demanding of the skills a fisherman delights in. They are special places, ever changing with the tide's movements, full of the special life of the sea's meeting with the land. One grows to know them gradually, in rain and fog and sunshine, in wind and calm, at dawn and dusk; and as knowledge builds to intimacy the dramatic values are plain at last, richer and stronger than the simple splendor the child's mind hoped to discover.

2. *Patterns and Problems*

From time to time I decide that I am going to learn some estuary thoroughly—unravel its tidal patterns, solve the movements and preferences of its fish, understand it completely. It is a very nice decision to make and a most pleasant one to work on. It becomes necessary, of course, to fish the chosen estuary as often as possible, at varying stages of varying tides and at all seasons of the year, all times of day; so far I have managed to resist the temptation of night fishing, though I am sure it could be productive. At first one learns very fast. Patterns emerge, theories seem proved, real understanding, even total solution seem almost in sight. At about that stage, most of it all falls apart. Patterns seem suddenly more complex and less recognizable. Theories disprove themselves. Some understanding remains but total solution is far out of sight. I never feel regretful about this or particularly surprised; I suppose it all happens too gradually. Nor am I properly humbled, because it will only be a matter of time before I start out to solve some other fishing problem with much the same result. But I have usually had a wonderful time and occasional sensations of achievement.

I have undertaken to solve some fair-sized estuaries in my time, the Campbell and the Nimpkish among them, and I have often felt quite self-satisfied with the results. But generally I pick on smaller ones, in the mistaken conviction that they will prove quite easy and the solutions will be quick and complete. After all, what is there to solve but half a mile of channel less than a hundred feet wide at low tide? It is never quite the same channel for two consecutive hours, let alone two consecutive days, but one feels that this should not matter too much. An hour or two of fishing on most of the major variations, appropriately repeated at different seasons through the year, should reveal everything.

The last estuary I seriously attacked in this way belongs to a smallish creek I will call Cedar Creek. The creek comes from several small lakes, through a series of falls, then flattens out into a lively run of two or three miles to the sea. In these lower reaches the pale amber water, averaging perhaps thirty or forty feet wide, supports good spawning runs of pink salmon and cutthroat trout and smaller runs of coho salmon and winter steelhead. I know of very few creeks of this size and length that are more productive, but it has a happy combination of good spawning gravels with slow flat reaches of nursing water, and the lakes help to prevent excessive floods in fall and winter or extremely low water in dry periods.

I knew the creek fairly well before reaching my arrogant

decision to solve all its moods. It comes to its estuary in a fast run over a bed of heavy boulders and two deep rocky pools that the flood tides reach. Below the second of these it spreads over a gravelly shallow and accepts a tiny creek from a small meadow on the right bank, before gathering itself into a well-defined channel over mud and sand flats that are exposed for a quarter of a mile or more at extreme low tides. The flats end in a shelving drop-off into a wide bay beyond narrow beds of eelgrass, through which the creek makes a rippling flow at low-water slack.

In previous years I had made some fair catches of good-sized cutthroats in both spring and fall, usually at low water on long run-outs. I had picked up occasional cohos and coho jacks in the fall and twice, in October, I had made excellent catches of cutthroats as the tide flooded over the wide gravel bar just below the meadow; these were big harvest cutthroats, averaging about two pounds, and were probably moving up into the stream to ripen and spawn by Christmas or soon after.

What I had really hoped to do was get some fairly clear idea of the movements of such fish as these throughout much of the year. Undoubtedly they went fairly well out into the sea at times and clearly enough they came into the mouth of the creek at times—behind the salmon in October, for instance, and as the fry run came down in late April and May. But it seemed highly probable that they came into the estuary or near it at other times as well.

As usual, the early stages were quite rewarding. In the course of periodic visits during the summer months I found a few feeding fish off the mouth of the channel at low tide and along the eelgrass beds on either side. Following on around the edge of the bay, I was able to find them again off the rock bluffs and out from the gravel beaches over a mile from the creek mouth. They seemed to be few and rather widely scattered, cutthroats with some smaller Dolly Vardens among them. But they were particularly handsome and well-conditioned fish and their colors noticeably reflected their salt-water environment. In parts of the bay, for instance, the kelp and other weeds have an unusual turquoise sheen and the fish from such places very plainly reflected this color in their fins and along their backs; this suggested that they were not ranging very widely, as the fish I caught off the creek mouth and along the eelgrass beds near it had a greenish color and no sign of blue.

I knew the fishing would pick up as fall approached, and towards the middle of August I began to go to the creek more often, testing the intermediate tides as well as the extreme lows. Almost immediately I realized I had a fine unsolved fishing problem right at hand. The cutthroats I had been catching around the bay and off the mouth of the creek had been good ones, usually fifteen or sixteen inches long and most of them maturing to spawn in the coming winter. They were hard to find, but usually took the fly fairly readily and faithfully once I had found them. But in the tidal channel of the creek there were always a few smaller fish, around ten or twelve inches, extremely active, certain to follow the fly at least once if they saw it, but very difficult indeed to hook. Because they were small I had passed on without bothering them too much. Now it was suddenly clear to me that these really *were* estuary fish, probably a year younger than those out in the bay, but spending their whole time feeding in the channel and over the mud flats on either side of it as the tide flooded over them.

Cutthroats in estuaries are nearly always quite difficult fish to convince, probably because most estuaries hold an abundance of natural food of various kinds. Occasionally one strikes on just the right pattern of fly or just the right way of working it, or both, and all goes very well indeed. Far more often one sees fish feeding, covers them, and is rewarded by a follow, a timid pull, a halfhearted rise, sometimes nothing at all. So, I told myself, it was highly important to go to work on the little resident fish. If I could learn to take them regularly, I should be ready when the larger fish moved in from the bay.

In estuary fishing one is likely to lean fairly heavily on silver-bodied flies for the obvious reason that small fish of one kind or another are likely to be available to the trout—salmon migrants, sculpins, perch and rock-cod fry, needle-fish, even small herrings are commonly in the stomachs of estuary fish. I had caught a few of the small cutthroats on silver-bodied flies, but I had little faith in them because for every fish I hooked, half a dozen followed the fly and either missed it or turned away without being hooked. The next most likely possibility are the gammarids, the sand hoppers or sand fleas that are abundant everywhere. I had tried my usual imitations, again without any convincing results. The spruce fly, often very good for estuary cut-throats, did not interest them. Occasionally, on the higher stages of flood tide, the little fish dimpled quietly at the surface and I had taken a few on floating flies; but they moved a good deal and were hard to cover and usually hard to reach. Besides, it was obvious that most of the time they were not feeding at the surface at all.

Along the edges of the Cedar Creek estuary there are great numbers of small, transparent mysid shrimps throughout the summer months. Most of them are about half an inch long or less, slightly humped and with regular black speckling along the back. The little cutthroats often came into the shallows at the edge of the flooding tide where these tiny shrimps were massed in thousands, and I began to suspect that the answer might be here.

The first attempt I made at imitating these little creatures was the most successful, and since the fly has proved effective for other types of fish under quite varying conditions, it seems worth giving the dressing:

Hook size: 10–14.	Hackle: Sparse natural
Tag: Orange tying silk.	blue, soft.
Tail: 5 strands of tippet.	Wings: 2 slender strips of
Body: Silver tinsel.	barred summer duck.

The body was rather short for the hook size, and I hoped that its silver, with the lightly barred wing feathers, might give some illusion of transparency. On its first trial this fly securely hooked three of the small fish in quick succession, and I felt that the problem was solved; within an hour it had also taken a sixteen-inch coho jack and a cutthroat of about the same size and I was inclined to believe I had solved all estuary problems for all time. I named the fly the Mysid and tied some more like it, willfully disregarding the fact that the three small fish I had killed had only asellus, the underwater sow bugs, in their stomachs. After all, I had found the little shrimps in the stomachs of other fish, which made it reasonable enough to suppose that my fly had been taken for a fairly faithful imitation.

My solution proved to be a very temporary affair. The Mysid fly continued to be quite effective, but I learned that fish could follow it and turn away or swirl at it and miss it and my percentage of solidly hooked fish was not a great deal better than with any other fly. The solution, I decided, was not in mysid, but in asellus. The decision had a faintly reminiscent ring—it seemed to recall an earlier idea that nothing more than a really good sand-hopper imitation was needed to catch estuary cutthroats under any and all conditions—but I did not let this discourage me.

Asellus is a close aquatic relative of the terrestrial sow bug or wood louse that one finds nearly everywhere in rotting wood. Like the wood louse, it crawls many-footed and clings to slivers of wood and bark; threatened, it rolls itself into a defensive ball. Unlike the wood louse, it swims under water, quite swiftly and effectively, on its back, and this presumably is when the cutthroats find it, though they may also pick it off rocks and waterlogged wood, as they do snails and caddis larvae. Its color is usually a dull olive, though this may vary to slate-blue or orange.

My imitation was a bulky olive seal's fur body, ribbed with gold wire. Over the back of this I set strands of peacock sword, tied in at head and tail, and to give the whole thing life and movement in the water I wound on a good-sized, soft, badger hackle behind the eye of the hook. Again, the fly was an immediate success and again this early success tapered off from the dramatic to the normal. Like the Mysid, the Asellus is a good, solid, effective pattern

that I still tie and use often. Both flies take estuary cutthroats quite well at times and both have also taken cohos
and pink salmon in estuaries; but it is equally true that both
have taken fish well in fresh water, miles away from any
natural mysids or asellus, and I find myself wondering
whether the estuary cutthroats take them because they look
a little bit like the creatures they are supposed to represent,
or simply because they are there in front of them and look
like something that might be good to eat.

Little excitements with special patterns such as these
are only a small part of the pleasure of learning about an
estuary, or any other form of fly-fishing. They never really
solve anything, but no true fisherman will admit that fish
have a right to miss or turn away from his flies. He may
at times blame low water or bright sun or some other condition beyond his control, but he supposes that his fly looks
like something the fish wants to eat; it is rejected only
because its movement or its appearance is unconvincing.
At times this is undoubtedly so, but there are also times
and conditions that can make fish behave very uncertainly
with natural prey.

Seeing the mysid shrimps massed in their thousands along
the edges of tidal water and knowing that the trout do
take them, I have often wondered why they are not under
constant attack. They seem totally defenseless and should
be a most attractive type of feed. Last year I introduced a
number of them into a small aquarium with several coho
fingerlings, thinking they would be readily caught. The
cohos were enthusiastic, but totally ineffective. The tiny
shrimps swam gently about and the cohos dashed at them.
The shrimps held their way or their station until the fishes'

jaws were within half an inch of them, then flicked their humped, transparent bodies upwards, downwards or to either side—just far enough to evade the rush. A few were caught, usually by a second fish in evading the first. But within minutes the little cohos became so frustrated and discouraged that they would scarcely bother to attack. Later, as the shrimps weakened in the fresh water of the aquarium, they were more easily caught and within twelve hours all had disappeared. I repeated the experiment several times, and each time it was the same. The evasive reaction is so effective and so precise that I suspected it might be tactile rather than visual, perhaps a response to compression of the water in front of the attacker's rush. But since one gets the same result by poking a finger against the outside of the aquarium glass, I assume it must be visual. In either case, it may well explain the highly uncertain response of estuary trout to the mysid imitation.

It does not take much imagination to extend this principle to the sand hoppers and to asellus. Both these creatures are at home crawling on the bottom, and the sand hoppers can even jump under water. When they decide to swim, their mid-water journeys are usually short and erratic, quickly returning again to the comparative safety of the bottom. A fish must respond very quickly to catch them and undoubtedly many escape, since both answer any attack by attempted evasion.

If one compares all this with the behavior of fresh-water forage, the differences are obvious. The nymphs of most May flies, stone flies and sedges are seldom found in mid-water except during their brief journey from bottom to surface, when it is time to break out their wings. Their

swimming powers are relatively feeble and their means of
evasion are practically nonexistent. A trout can approach
these creatures calmly and confidently, certain of their
capture; much of the time he need only hold in the water
while they are drifted to him by the current. The trout of
the estuaries has many more opportunities to find feed, but
he also has many more opportunities to miss and feel foolish
or to bump his nose against the bottom in pursuit; he must
be ready to make a sudden chase, but ready also to make a
still more sudden change of direction, perhaps four or five
if he is trying to catch a mysid. It seems reasonable to suppose that this accounts for much of the finicky and difficult
response of estuary trout.

Not that a fly-fisherman can be expected to leave it at
that. If he is satisfied his pattern is as good as it can be,
he must begin to wonder about the way he is fishing it.
Can it be given some motion or some illusion of behavior
that is nearer to the performance of the creature it represents? Should it be fished deep or near the surface? Should
it move from deep water to shallow or from shallow to
deep? With the current, across it or against it? Again, one
develops many fine theories and one day seems to prove
them, the next to deny them. But for Cedar Creek I learned
two lessons that are still of value. The small resident fish
nearly always took a fly that was moving fairly rapidly
from deep to shallow. But the larger fish—cutthroats over
two pounds, cohos, coho jacks and pink salmon—again and
again took the fly at the limit of the cast, as I was allowing
it to settle to useful fishing depth, before it had been given
any artificial movement at all.

These are among the technical issues that estuary fishing

raises. One does not so much solve them as come to terms with them. One works at them under constantly changing conditions of tide and flow and light and the subtle movements of the fish within the tide. There are few more demanding tests of a wet-fly fisherman's skill and knowledge and few forms of fishing where one can expect such a variety of good game fish. But I think its strongest fascination may well be in the intensity of observation it encourages and the sense of intimacy that grows from this close watch upon the infinity of tiny factors that make it.

3. *Solutions and Surmises*

Fly patterns and the techniques of using them are not really the major concerns of the estuary fisherman, though he may devote a good deal of time and attention to them. His most urgent interest is in the movements of the fish. What rhythms do they follow and repeat? What can he expect from the tides at all their different heights and stages? What will be the influence of a set of wind? What do the successive seasons bring as the year moves on?

Without some sort of theories and thoughts on such matters estuary fishing has very little meaning; one may be lucky and find fish, or unlucky and not find them, exactly as may happen on a river or lake or out in the sea itself. In estuary fishing the fish are always moving. Even on a familiar estuary the fisherman is always wondering: where are they now? Have they come in yet? Have they gone on past me? Have they turned into the slough or spread over the flat? The answers to such questions is in testing the few favored spots, upstream or down, where the fish usually hold a little longer and feed a little more freely than elsewhere. Each time he finds the fish, everything seems gained. He notes the time and the stage of the tide, the set of the wind, the state of the water. Probably he kills a fish or two, misses others and promises himself he will be back tomorrow, just about an hour later, to find them promptly and make a killing. Tomorrow comes, as all tomorrows do, and the fisherman is there. There is a good chance the fish will be there, too, but they may not be, for estuaries do not solve themselves so predictably as this.

Yet this is the manner of learning and there really is no other. At times the fish break the surface in feeding or show their whereabouts by jumping, but more often they slip quietly by on the tide, feeding well down in the water. One learns what to expect, but not necessarily what will happen. Fortunately, expectation is all a fisherman needs to take him out.

Cedar Creek was no exception to all these rules. The estuary has a tidal range of over fourteen feet, which makes for plenty of variety. I learned to follow down the channel on the last of the ebb and expect feeding fish somewhere along the way. I learned to distrust low-water slack because the fish, if one could find them then, often seemed lazy and hesitant, following rather than taking. As the tide flooded, fish were likely to follow somewhere behind its front, moving rather quickly through the lower reaches of the channel, pausing to feed in the deep water by the broken piles, then moving on to the standing piles farther upstream.

On the mid-stages of big tides the flood at Cedar Creek has a violent reversal, running in fiercely for a few minutes, raising the water level by a foot or more, then tearing out again just as fast and seemingly just as far. I don't care much for this irrational violence and I don't think the fish do either, because I have never caught them well at such times. But there have been several times when I have saved a frustrating afternoon by picking up three or four good fish as the tide built up towards full flood in the two rocky pools at the mouth of the creek.

This sort of knowledge is interesting and useful. It is by no means exact and is quite unlikely to work miracles, but it gives direction and purpose to the search that an estuary fisherman is nearly always making and it adds to itself continually. Quite insignificant marks—a point of weed, the level of the tide on a rock, a curl of water behind some obstruction—become echoes of experience, to be tested faithfully and hopefully.

Estuary fishing, quite plainly, has its special seasons and for most fishermen these are enough—the clear-cut movement of both trout and salmon in the fall, the feeding movement of the cutthroats as the fry come down in spring. But once one has set out to solve an estuary, they are no longer enough. After all, there are trout somewhere about in every month of the year and one should be able to find them; more than this, as intimacy grows one begins to feel an affectionate, even a jealous, curiosity about those other months and times.

In the estuaries of the larger streams one does find fish, and find them well, in almost any month of the year. The smaller streams are a lot more difficult and uncertain, which is natural enough as they offer much less range to feeding fish. I have tried Cedar Creek estuary in every month of the year, but have never found fish there in any numbers except briefly in the spring and again in late summer and fall. The easy explanation is that most of the fish move up into the creek with the salmon, to feed as the salmon spawn and to spawn themselves later. Certainly they do go up the creek in good numbers and one can catch them there if one cares to fight the brush. But they do not all spawn every year and by December most of the salmon are dead, so there can be little feed to keep them in the creek unless they are spawning.

One September day I had come to the creek early in the morning and had done well on the ebbing tide—that is, I had a coho salmon and two good big cutthroats to show for myself. Salmon were showing out in the bay and the cutthroats were hanging somewhere in the drop-off at the mouth of the creek's tidal channel; one or two had followed the fly and refused it when I first came down there, but now they were not moving at all so I turned back across the flats to wait for the flood tide. There was, as always at Cedar Creek estuary, plenty to see and enjoy. Tall gray herons were standing patiently in the shallow water just off the flats. An osprey worked out from shore, swinging high over the bay to circle back in the hope of finding some unwary fish near the surface. Bonaparte's gulls, small and graceful, were rafted on the slack water, talking gently among themselves and waiting for the tide.

Beyond the mouth of the bay small boats were using the turn of the tide to pass the turbulence of the narrows.

As I came back towards the big rock where I had left my lunch and my fish I noticed a strange little party come down to the first of the tidal pools. I made them out as a man and three women, moving very slowly, apparently searching for something among the rocks. I was curious, because I could think of nothing worth searching for. It was too far up for clams or crabs, there were few mussels at the stream mouth. It crossed my mind that they might be Indians planning to build a tidal fish trap, but it seemed unlikely. No Indian had used the stream within my memory of it. It was a mild relief to see, as I came closer, that the man and one of the women had started to fish, while the other two women settled to watch. I gave them no chance at all of fish where they were at that stage of the tide, but summer people often do fish in very strange places and seem quite happy about it.

The man came down to me as I was eating my lunch. He was short and thickset, about fifty, and his walk was clumsy and uncomfortable over the rocks and the slippery surface of the flat. I judged him to be from shop or factory, not from the woods, but he was friendly and much interested to see my fish. I thought his face vaguely familiar.

"I used to live up here until 1938," he said. "Fished the creek a lot then."

We talked of how it had been in the thirties, of the big logging camp at the mouth of the creek, of the footbridge across the creek and the log dump now rotted away to a few worm-eaten piles. We tried each other out on names, in the usual way of men who have worked in or around the camps. Bosses like Eric Lund, Hank Phelan, Bernie Blakely, Tom Daly were easy enough—we both knew them. But when I tried rigging men like Blondy Anderson, Dunc Thew, Tommy Dickinson, he shook his head.

"I always worked in the car shops, down at the Beach," he said. "But I've seen you before somewhere."

"Maybe at the strike camp in '34," I suggested.

"Could be," he agreed. "I was down there some." We left it at that and returned to the creek and its fishing. "We're too early for the tide," he said. "But I've had some wonderful fishing as it begins to surge into those pools."

"Was that your place up at the edge of the meadow?" I asked, pointing to the remains of a small house in what had once been a carefully tended vegetable garden.

"No, I lived across the footbridge alongside the tracks. Used to come down to the creek all the time. Those were hard days, back in the thirties. Getting down here for a spell of fishing was as good as two weeks' rest. Made a new man out of a guy."

"Did you find fish all through the year?" I asked.

"Pretty near any time. I been down here in three feet of snow on Christmas Day and had fifteen trout in two hours; not big ones, mind, ten or twelve inches, but it's all a man could ask."

"It's still pretty good," I said. "But I've never found them like that in the winter."

"It'll keep good, just so people don't find out and pile in. Off the old footbridge, now, I've watched 'em many a time. The salmon schooling up and big trout in rows behind them."

I made the most of my opportunity and questioned him

about everything he had seen and found out in the years
he had lived by the creek. He was a consistent worm fisherman, which meant that some of the information needed
re-interpretation in terms of what a fly might be able to do.
He was often vague about dates and other details, but
much of what he said went to the movements of the fish
and I could find in it new reason to search again in the
months that had produced little for me. I asked about steelhead and he said he had seen them from the footbridge
but had never hooked one.

So I fished the estuary again in November, December,
January and February and found very little. I fished only
on occasional days and perhaps gave up too easily. Once or
twice I found a few small trout in the channel. In a thick
December snowstorm I hooked two fresh steelhead in quick
succession in the first of the tidal pools. From time to time
I plowed upstream through the brush to the fresh-water
pools and the trout were there—in November, it seemed,
mostly large ones of two or three pounds, in mid-December
many more of them, but smaller, around a pound or a
pound and a half. When they had passed through the estuary I still do not know, nor have I yet found the quantities
of ten- and twelve-inch fish my friend found there that
Christmas Day in the thirties.

So I am still very far from solving Cedar Creek estuary.
But I have a pretty good working knowledge of it. Today,
for instance, a day towards mid-June of 1963, sunny and
windy, with a favorable tide in the middle of the day, I
went down there to test past experience and refresh my
memory a little. I warned myself that I could expect nothing in the way of fish except the ten- or twelve-inch resi-

dents unless the tide was low enough to work easily out to the bluffs—I had no intention of doing anything hard. The life of the estuary would be active otherwise; the mysids would be there in their thousands, asellus would be working around near bottom, birds would be moving freely and the whole place would have a feeling of freshness and future promise that is subtly changed in the maturity of fall.

I was later than I had intended to be and the tide was near low-water slack as I walked out over the flats. The wind was strong and violent and wave action had stirred the water to muddiness for some distance up the channel and all along the eelgrass above the drop-off. I thought it a set of unlikely fishing conditions, but the tide was low enough to work round to the bluffs. Once there I realized, as I had before, that I do not much care for fishing from them. Today they were dark in the shade with their clinging starfish and crawling asellus; the wind was full in my face and the water was dark and uneasy. I made a few casts with rapidly waning enthusiasm. Though I was reaching out over good water, nothing moved to the fly. I saw that the tide was making on the rocks and thought the sunny flats a far better place to be. A Dolly Varden of about fourteen inches chased the fly right to my feet, missed it in a wild dash and disappeared while I was still thinking how pretty he looked. I rolled out another cast, hooked him and lost him almost immediately. From that I worked back towards the creek channel, killing time by making occasional casts across the eelgrass beds towards the drop-off. It is rarely a productive operation, and this day was no exception.

I was still too early for the tide in the channel, but I

fished up it anyway—as one should, if only in the hope of learning something new. The mysids were thick along the edge of the water, so I changed from the long-hooked streamer to my little imitation. Nothing moved from the deep water by the cut-off piles, and I kept moving up to where the standing piles no longer stand and the creek flow was shallow and plain. Then a little silvery fish jumped out down by the cut-off piles. I worked carefully down and hooked him or another like him fifty feet or so upstream from his jump. He was just over twelve inches long and rather thin. Ten minutes later I found a slightly larger fish near the cut-off piles and had the fly come away just as I was going to beach him. I changed then from the little Mysid imitation to the Asellus and a third fish took securely. Three small fish swam quickly towards me in the sunlight, very near the surface, turned back and disappeared into the deep water beyond the pile stubs. But no other fish came to the fly, so I turned away to eat lunch by the big rock and consider whether I would wait for the tide to flood into the pools.

Sitting there, I realized how many other things I knew about the Cedar Creek estuary. It was no surprise to count the six great blue herons stalking the edge of the tide on the far side of the stream. When the osprey swung out over the treetops and across the bay towards Nymph Cove I expected him, and expected, too, his circle back and careful hunting. The kingfishers were fairly quiet in their fishing; later in the year when the young are out of the nest and perched on the big rocks of the creek bed waiting to be fed they become very noisy indeed. A merganser came down the creek with her young and two drakes, still in full plumage, swung in and settled over the flooded eel-grass as though they had never seen her before. In the fall, waders and sandpipers are generally among my company on the flats, but today the nearest to them was a killdeer with a nest somewhere above the meadow. Bald eagles circled over the trees towards Race Point, and a small flock of Bonaparte's gulls, early arrivals, moved up over the flat with the tide.

When I went down to the edge of the water to collect some of the mysid shrimps for the aquarium, hermit crabs were crawling everywhere among the rocks. The sea grasses in the meadow and along the far bank were brilliantly green, changing through a thousand shades as they blew like silk in the wind. The wind was freshening steadily with the tide, and I gave up the idea of fishing again. Walking back towards the road through the grasses, I found chocolate fritillaria lilies blooming everywhere at my feet and band-tailed pigeons were clattering out of the maples. These things I had not noticed at the creek before, but now they became part of my knowledge of it. The rest was familiar and richer in value for its familiarity; even the fish had been much as I had expected them to be, though June is not a month I know well there and I had picked the day and the tide at random. One does not solve estuaries; one comes to know them and this is enough.

4. *Behind the Salmon*

WHEN THE SALMON TURN INTO THE estuary of a small stream one has a right to expect that some big cutthroat trout will be near them. Often they are, but often, too, they can be quite hard to find. Then, particularly if it is late in the season, one is likely to get an uneasy feeling that they have all moved up into the creek and that fishing the estuary may be a waste of time.

I know much better than to go up into the lower reaches of Cedar Creek and try to fish them, even though there are several pools that hold both cutthroats and steelheads really well. These pools are long and slow, for the most part too deep to wade and with steep, slippery clay banks that support tangled crab-apple thickets on one side and overhanging alders on the other side. Any kind of a backcast is out of the question and even a roll or spey cast is grossly inhibited by the precarious stance and crowding brush; it must also find a way into the water between the overhanging limbs. Inevitably one accepts all this and makes a cast or two. Just as inevitably, all goes well at first, one falls into easy admiration of the accurate and tidy way in which the fly settles close under the hazards of the far bank, its cunning search of likely places, the precariously smooth roll that sets it out again to search again. Then, and it can happen in various ways, from a slip on the clay bottom that fills waders to a hang-up in a high branch that catches the peak of the roll, all the ease and smoothness goes out of things and one recalls the forsaken resolve to stay away from such places.

As recently as last fall I found things too slow in Cedar Creek estuary and decided to take a quick look up the creek in the hope of finding a good fish or two to round out the day. It was well on in October and I knew that a strong run of humpback salmon had moved in, so it was reasonable to suppose the estuary cutthroats had all moved up behind them.

The head of the long pool is not too bad a place to get at. After a wild struggle with the crab apples I found my-self in the water at the head of the pool, fairly securely placed and with a nice space between the alder limbs inviting my fly to a strongish run on the far side. The creek was flowing well with good fall water, dark but clear, and past experience suggested I should find the first fish twenty or thirty yards further downstream, probably near my own bank where the current spread. I had put up a Harger's Orange, one of several I had tied with claret-colored hair in the wing instead of orange a few years before and a fly I like particularly well for fall cutthroats as well as steelhead. It rolled out nicely, settled into the

water and was immediately chased and taken by a fine
cutthroat of about three pounds.

At this stage I wasn't really fishing—just getting my fly
out. I did set the hook, but then I stood like a particularly
dull-witted sheep while the fish ran off downstream. There
was an impressive tangle of brush against my bank about
forty yards downstream; before I came to and started to
move, the line was well tangled in it and the fish was jumping below.

I had sense enough to forget him and work my way
carefully downstream—after all, he could only break the
leader and if he chose instead to lie quietly I might even
be able to disentangle the line and tighten up on him again.
The tangle was worse than I had expected, but I struggled
with it in admirable calm, freed the worst of it with no
more harm than my right arm wet to the armpit and saw
my empty fly trailing in the current below. It was a mild
disappointment, because it is always satisfying to free a
mess of this sort and find that the fish has waited through
one's patient efforts, but I knew very well I had earned
nothing better—that recovering the fly was a good deal
more than I deserved.

For a moment I considered working on down the pool
from the brush pile, but that seemed wrong since I had
made only one cast at the head of the pool, so I worked
my way back up again to where I had started. I placed
myself carefully, repeated my first cast exactly, watched
my fly settle again nearly between the alder branches and
began to think of the next cast and the next after that,
when I might reasonably expect to find another fish. Then
I saw the fish shouldering across behind the fly, an exact

double of the one I had just lost. He took, I tightened; two minutes later my line was tangled in the same brush pile and I was floundering down, by no means calmly, to free it again. And again the fish was lost but the fly was there. In the end I did hook and kill a good fish far below the brush pile, almost at the tail of the pool, but I solemnly renewed all my resolutions about avoiding the crab apples and clay banks and other humiliations of Cedar Creek's most productive pools.

The next day I went about forty miles down along the coast of Vancouver Island to look at several small creeks and their estuaries, among them Sedge Creek. The sensible way to Sedge Creek estuary is to wade down the gravel bed of the creek itself from the highway bridge. It is clear and comfortable going, and one can make an occasional cast to where the creek deepens on a bend or under a root.

Just below the highway bridge the creek bed has been deepened by a bulldozer for several hundred yards to give the flood water an open, easy channel. To break the flow still more and prevent washing of the gravel there are heavy cross logs set into the high gravel banks at intervals of fifty or sixty yards. Behind these, long shallow pools of gently flowing water with a few deeper spots make good lying places for dog and coho salmon—and sometimes cutthroats.

On this particular day there was a school of some twenty or thirty dog salmon in the upper pool, big fish, moving a little, calm and lazy. There was every possible chance that a few cutthroats were lying somewhere amongst them, so I kept as well back from the water as I could and began to drop my Harger's Orange as nearly as I could behind individual members of the scattered, shifting school. Every

so often a fish would move up under the swing of the fly
and I would feel the fly or the leader scrape against him,
but I slacked carefully at such times and for a while all
went well. Then the inevitable happened. A fish moved
up under the fly almost as it landed. For a moment of time
Harger's Orange was swinging freely across the current,
a moment later it had stopped, securely set in the dorsal
fin of a fifteen-pound dog salmon.

At first neither I nor the fish was greatly concerned. I
thought I should get my fly back without too much difficulty, he didn't think the slight restraint of the line was
particularly significant. He began to swim slowly upstream.
I left the line slack, hoping the fly would come free. Near
the head of the pool he turned and began to swim, still
quite slowly, downstream. I decided to tighten, again in
the hope that the fly would come free. My fish resented
this and swam a little harder, taking line nicely and stirring
up the other fish in the pool. By the time he turned, just
above the cross log at the tail, most of them were following
him. By the time he had swum his majestic way back to
the head of the pool they were tightly schooled around
him, sympathetic or curious or both or neither.

The next trip down the pool was a lot faster and at the
tail he broke with some violence, the school all about him
still. He liked it down there and I had some difficulty in
persuading him to come back up. In the end he came, the
whole school still with him. And so it went on, up and
down the pool, the school so closely together that it seemed
I had hooked twenty fish at once on my single poor little
fly. And my one fish felt like twenty. I had to accept that
he was not tiring in the slightest and that my little eight-

foot rod was not going to bring him to beach or to hand within the foreseeable future. I tried my best, because I was really quite fond of that fly. I could direct him a little, turn him at the tail of the pool, even force him to break water, but that was about all. In the end I pointed the rod at him and broke.

Although I had kept fairly well back from the edge of the water throughout the performance, it seemed certain that the pool must be completely disturbed, so I climbed the high gravel bank on the left and started down it. I kept back in the shade of the timber, though, and watched curiously, because I wanted to see how the salmon settled down and how the fish behaved with my fly still in his dorsal fin. I found him easily, with the claret of hackle and wing in the fly showing up nicely, and he seemed just as calm as the others still schooled around him. They were already beginning to spread out through the pool and their movements were slow and lazy. As I turned my eyes from them to search the lower part of the pool I found the quiet, still shapes of two good cutthroats under the overhanging limbs of a small fir, some sixty feet up from the cross log.

These were the fish I had hoped to find among the salmon. They were flat on the bottom now, unmoving and apparently uninterested in anything about them. But it was not the sort of chance one passes up without a try of some sort. I drew farther back into the brush and circled carefully around to the tail of the pool.

My first guess was a good big floating fly. The larger fish of the two was lying a little farther out and a little downstream, so I put it over him, accurately and carefully, with a right-hand curve cast that kept the leader upstream of the drifting fly. Neither fish made the slightest move and though I repeated the cast a dozen times I could not detect even the quiver of a fin to give me encouragement.

My next thought was a nymph, but I discarded this in favor of an orange fly with a weighted body. I aimed for the same right-hand curve cast, but forgot to allow for the reduced air resistance and greater weight of the new fly. It overshot badly and whipped round into a left-hand curve that dropped it in midstream, at least eight feet over from where the fish was lying. He moved like a flash the second it touched the water and took perfectly. I tightened, held him for a second or two, then the fly came away. To my surprise he returned at once to his old position, though the second fish had disappeared.

It seemed a safe assumpiton that I had mistimed the strike in the surprise of seeing him come so far for the fly. To expect him to take again was totally unreasonable, but I threw the fly up anyway. It landed about six inches to his left and a foot upstream of him, and again he was on it the second it touched the water. This time I was certain of my strike. He was a strong, very fast fish of rather over two pounds, but I controlled him after two or three good runs and moved to a favorable spot to beach him, just above the cross log. As I brought him in there, the fly came away. This time I looked at the fly and found that the point and barb were broken off, no doubt by touching the rocks of the high gravel banks on a backcast.

The lesson is, I suppose, that if you are as careless a fisherman as I seem to be you should stay away from the upstream reaches of the small creeks. If you do not, they will certainly temper your pride, test your vocabulary and perhaps humiliate you in other unforeseen ways. But in the fall they hold some very good fish and the slightly larger ones like Cedar Creek and Sedge Creek may present some very pretty and interesting situations. Any resolve to stay away is only good for a few days. One can so easily make a counterresolve to be careful, respectful, farsighted and extremely skillful. Beside this the frustrations of entangling brush, slippery banks and limited casting room fade into insignificant memory. Pride is completely restored and all is ready for the next fall.

5. *Perfect Morning*

I SEEM TO HAVE BUILT SUCH A SERIES OF difficulties, accidents and failures around my account of the small streams and their estuaries that the sum is more pain than pleasure. But I am sure it will discourage no one. Enlarging upon the difficulties of his sport is as natural as breathing to any fisherman, and only the unkindest and most perspicacious of our critics bother to tell us that we are busily seeking to enlarge our own prestige as we do so. Certainly fishing is a difficult and exacting sport; why would we bother with it otherwise? And just as certainly there are days when everything goes smoothly and well for us, even in estuaries and small creeks, thus proving beyond a shadow of doubt that our wit, wisdom, skill and cunning are fully equal to those of the smartest fish that swims.

Cedar Creek has given me some very good days indeed, and some of the best of them have brought real surprises. Surprises are a good part of estuary fishing, but usually they come one at a time. An early September morning at Cedar Creek five or six years ago brought me several in quick succession.

I got down to the creek at about six-thirty of a misty morning, with about two hours of ebb tide before low-water slack. As I came out on to the flats a few humpbacks were showing in the upper reaches of the channel. A dowitcher and two yellowlegs were feeding at the edge of the creek, and I could hear the flight and talk of ducks and gulls out in the bay. It was very still, with overcast above the light mist, and the water was gray in the thin light. A heron, briefly seen, looked enormous as he flapped towards the far side of the creek.

I started below where the humpbacks were showing, fishing the small Mysid fly on a 2x leader. At the second or third cast a fish followed the fly, swirled at it and missed. The same thing happened again a few moments later; I guessed they were cutthroats of fairly good size. On the next cast I let the fly settle for a few seconds; on the recovery there was a good follow, a heavy swirl and I was fast in a fish. He jumped almost as soon as the hook was home, and I saw he was very bright, probably about five pounds. His first run took thirty or forty yards of backing, fast and so close under the surface that I could almost see his shape. When he turned I recovered the backing and about half the fly line, but he ran into the backing three more times before he began to tire, each time fast and close to the surface, jumping whenever he chose. I finally beached him, a coho of just over six pounds, lightly hooked in the corner of the jaw.

A few casts later another fish took my fly solidly, jumped

once and fell back on his belly, then again straight out and down on his tail. For a moment I thought he might be another coho, but I had seen a touch of yellow on his brightness, and his slower, deeper rushes soon persuaded me he was a cutthroat. He was an unusually fine one for the creek, twenty inches and a full three and a half pounds.

There is nothing better than a good quick start of this sort. One has enough fish on the beach to justify one's existence as a fisherman, with all the rest of the day ahead to fish as one pleases without the slightest obligation to produce results. The mist had lifted now and the overcast was breaking up. A little breeze had started out in the bay, and I had plenty of time to watch the movement of scaups and scoters and goldeneyes, cormorants, herons and gulls. Half a dozen killer whales were surfacing and blowing with majestic slowness near the far shore. The osprey was still fishing and, as usual, was successful. He shook the water from his wings, pointed his fish head forward, then swept his way over the treetops and on up the creek. I worked slowly down along the channel, watching a big coho jumping again and again out in the bay. He came crashing along just outside the weed beds, and for a moment I hoped he might turn in at the creek mouth, but he kept on going.

Without trying very hard I picked up a nice cutthroat of about sixteen inches and a precocious male coho of the same size, and let them both go. Then a heavy fish broke water on the far side, near the eelgrass. It was a feeding break, repeated almost immediately, and I saw a scatter of small fish ahead of it. I waded in as far as I could and just managed to reach the spot with a long cast. The fish took, or rather hit, the moment the fly landed and ran at once, then stopped almost as suddenly. I tried to move him again, but felt only dead weight. I tried slacking off the line, then renewing the strain from different directions, but nothing made any difference. It took me some little while to realize that my fish had dived into a thick bed of eelgrass, and when I did realize it I assumed that he was free of the fly and had left it hooked in the weed; no sea-run trout or salmon, in my experience, likes getting tangled in a weed bed or stays there long if he gets into one.

But this fish was still on. Some shift of current straightened out the eelgrass, the pull came directly on him again and he came thrashing to the surface. I tried to hold him up, but he was very strong and took out line in spite of me. The run was short, fast and down, into another bed of eelgrass but this time on my side of the channel. I worked him out of it slowly and laboriously, slopping water into my boots in the process. He was a large and very handsome rockfish, yellow with heavy black barring.

By this time I had worked down almost to the mouth of the channel and the tide was near low slack, so I began to reach out over the drop-off. Some good cutthroats were there, in the rippling flow from the creek mouth, but they seemed to be chasing the small fly without taking. The killer whales had moved in considerably, black backs and tall dorsal fins shining in the sun, the white of their underbellies showing occasionally as they rolled. I changed to a streamer fly while I was watching them and immediately hooked and returned three good cutthroats in quick suc-

cession, even though I was still dividing my attention between fishing and the intermittent surfacing of the whales.
Then I hooked a Dolly Varden of about fourteen inches.

That seemed about enough and the tide was flooding
noticeably, so I changed to a small fly again and turned
to fish back up the channel. Just as I did so I saw the ripples
of fish moving in on the far side. I cast to them, let my
fly settle briefly and was into a big, strong silvery fish as
soon as I moved it. She ran well, taking a lot of line, but
after that it was a rather slow, straining fight. The eelgrass again made trouble, but this fish liked it no better
than I did. I beached her after about fifteen minutes, a perfect fresh-run humpback female of six and a half pounds.

It struck me then that I was achieving rather a remarkable mixed bag; cutthroats, cohos, a Dolly Varden, the
rock cod and now a good humpback. It seemed that everything in the estuary was feeding freely and well. I didn't
really want anything more, but it was only normal to make
a cast or two as I walked back along the edge of the
channel. I hooked and released another coho jack and saw
one or two other sizable fish swirl at the fly, but did not
bother to work for them. Just before I came to the standing piles, where the sandy bottom of the channel ends
and the rocks of the creek bed begin, my fly checked
near bottom in mid-channel. I struck and quickly dragged
to the surface a beautifully marked staghorn sculpin about
twelve inches long. I have hooked one other at Cedar
Creek since that time, but it is certainly not a species I
expect to take with a fly. Rock cod are more likely pros-
pects, but I cannot recall having taken one right at the

surface before or having cast to surface signs of a feeding rock cod.

I suppose this quiet September morning was one of those rare and happy occasions in a fisherman's life when every fish is feeding eagerly and any sort of performance will produce a catch. I did not have that feeling about it at the time; it seemed to me I was working fairly hard for every fish I caught, with the exception of the three cut-throats that took the streamer off the mouth. These reminded me a little of another time at the same stage of tide when I took eight fish averaging over two pounds within half an hour, but they reminded me also of still other times when fish after fish had chased my fly high in the rippled, sunlit water and not a single one had taken firm hold. Certainly I did not take fullest advantage of the occasion, nor had I any slightest wish to do so. I could have fished harder and more carefully in the time I was there and I could have stayed on to work the flood tide all the way up the channel. Perhaps I should have, if only to learn whether the mood of the fish would change. But the strange thing is that I am perfectly satisfied I do know. There would have been a short lull on the beginning of the tide, I should have had a few halfhearted rises towards mid-tide and perhaps hooked a fish or two; after that a sense of frustration and perhaps another small fish or two towards the peak of the tide.

If this sounds much too all-knowing, it certainly is. Yet it has in it many echos of many days' experience on many estuaries. If I am wrong, my arrogance has cost me nothing for I had had my fill of responsive fish on that particular day and needed nothing more. If I am right, which is far more likely, I saved my brief and lively morning from tapering into the anticlimax of midday. Perhaps I should regret, in a formal way, my betrayl of the scientific method; but I do not regret the impulse—it was less than a decision—that has kept that morning sharp and clear in my memory.

PART FOUR

Steelhead and Low Water

1. *More Steelhead Mysteries*

In a general way, one can classify steelhead runs as "summer" and "winter." Winter-run fish are usually coming into the rivers from about December first until March fifteenth, and nearly all of them spawn before the end of April. On some streams a few fish run before December first and on many streams fresh fish enter after March fifteenth, but these latter, though clean and bright, are heavy with milt and roe.

Summer runs are a great deal more complicated and any generalizations one cares to make about them are necessarily cautious. In spite of the great worth and popularity of the steelhead as a game fish, very little scientific investigation of its life history and movements has been undertaken and publications are few. My own observation has been casual and usually connected with fishing, but I have checked it whenever possible by comparing notes with

other anglers and biologists. I still learn every year something new that makes me adjust my ideas.

"True" summer steelhead runs seem to occur only on
streams that have a good deal of canyon water or, failing
this, a number of safe, deep holding pools. This seems
natural enough, since the fish remain in fresh water a long
while, through extreme low-water periods, and without
such protective water the runs probably could not have
established themselves or survived. A true summer run,
in most British Columbia waters at all events and probably
elsewhere, is one that enters its spawning stream from mid-
July to late fall and holds over through the winter to
spawn in April—or about the same time as the winter-run
fish. Nearly all such runs are preceded by a few early
arrivals that run in late May and June, and it is possible
that some of the fish spawn before the following April,
even before the end of the year. Certainly I have found
kelts in late November and early December, but I suspect
these are not typical of true summer runs.

This brings me to the really complicating factor. Many
steelhead streams seem to have a few fish running in nearly
every month of the year. This is certainly true of the
Campbell, a river that has no true summer run by my
standards, but which always yields me a few fresh fish
during the summer and fall months. Besides its regular
winter run, the Campbell has a dependable May run of
small fish that spawn almost immediately and leave the river
very quickly. Through the rest of the year, from June
until November, it has only a few "casuals" that one may
or may not be able to find, though I am convinced they
are always there. Most of these have no more sexual de-

velopment than true summer-run fish and probably spawn
in April; they may be the remnants of a once strong
summer run or else the sparse survivors of a run that has
never been able to establish itself in strength; in either
event, it seems that the river is at present lacking in some
essential requirement for a strong summer run.

The Quinsam, a tributary of the Campbell, has a very
fine run of winter fish and a rather sparse run that matches
the Campbell run of small May spawners. The summer
flow is very low and the stream has no real canyon water;
so it seems unlikely that any steelhead run to it in the
summer months. But the Quinsam has a small tributary,
alternatively known as Cold Creek or Coal Creek, which
comes from underground seepage and has extremely even
flow and temperature throughout the year. Wandering
along this stream in mid-July last year, I was astonished to
see two dark fish of about six or seven pounds lying in the
stream. It was clear that they had spawned very recently
and I was certain they were steelheads. The male was
quite weak and angled across the current to the bank close
to where I was standing. I knelt down carefully and eased
forward until I could reach into the water to tail him. I
held him briefly across my knees, fully confirming that
he was a steelhead and measuring him against my hand as
about twenty-five inches long. Then I released him and he
immediately rejoined the female in midstream, though I
judged him to be completely spawned out.

I offer this account not to confuse the issue, but to give
some idea of the wide variety of distribution and seasonal
habit that can be expected in steelhead. Though Coal Creek
is a very small stream and always clear, and though I have

watched it fairly closely for many years, to find spawning
steelhead there in July was a complete surprise. I still do
not know if these were two wandering individuals or the
remnants of a run that had once been larger or the possible
progenitors of a run establishing itself. Though the creek
lacks significant areas of good spawning gravel, it clearly
has advantages of temperature and flow that would be
attractive to fish ripening to spawn at that time of year.
Perhaps it has attracted a few late-maturing individuals
from the May run of the Campbell and the Quinsam. However one attempts to explain it, the fact remains that July
is not a usual spawning month for steelhead. In most
streams the fry from July spawning would reach their free-
swimming stage in November or December, to face the
floods, falling temperatures and limited feed of winter.

There are a number of true summer steelhead streams
along the west coast of Vancouver Island, among them the
San Juan, the Nitinat, the Caycuse, the Stamp, the Ash and
the Heber, a tributary of the Gold. A few fish enter them
in May and June, the peak of the run probably comes in
early July and late fish run in September and October;
all, or nearly all, are probably April spawners. By the first
weeks of May the streams hold only a few very dark kelts.

At their best, these streams offer some of the most interesting and satisfying fly-fishing to be found anywhere.
Unquestionably there are a good many others like them
that good fly-fishermen have not yet reached and explored,
so one listens eagerly to any and all tales and rumors that
may suggest a new discovery.

Two or three years ago a fly-fishing friend told me of
a successful trip to the Moyeha River, at the head of a

remote inlet on the west side of the island. He had been there in July of a hot dry summer and had found a beautiful little stream, readily waded. Working up from the salt water, he had taken fish after fish on the dry fly, all of them "rainbows" of about three pounds, though a few larger fish that he judged as about six or seven pounds had broken him.

This was exactly the sort of story I was looking for. My friend's "rainbows" sounded to me like a true summer run of steelhead. It was inconceivable that the stream could support resident fish of that size. The fish were a little on the small size for a true summer run—those in the Heber, for instance, average just under five pounds and run up to at least nine pounds—but it was not hard to imagine factors that could account for this. The timing of the run was right; the location of the stream was well within range of the best summer-run streams; it was of a good size and type, with a cool summer flow from high mountain peaks. There was only one adverse factor: close examination of a detailed topographical map suggested that there was little or no accessible part of the river with steep canyon walls, but the best of maps can be deceptive on a point like this.

In early September of last year I flew over to the Moyeha with two friends and camped just above tidewater for three days. From there we searched the lower four or five miles of the river carefully and thoroughly. The river was low and easy to travel, with good gravel bars and long narrow pools. There were some fine cutthroats in the first pool above tidewater, and I had every confidence that we would find the steelhead schooled in groups of ten or twenty fish in the pools above, as one finds them in the other summer-run streams at that time. But search as we would, they were not there. On the first day I rose and missed one fish of about four pounds at the head of a rock-walled pool about a mile and a half above the mouth. It was certainly a steelhead. The next day we killed two fish about three or four miles upstream, both of them males almost ready to spawn, both feeding heavily on anything the river had to offer—caddis, snails and drifting huckleberries—both about three and a half pounds. Though we looked closely into many of the deep and attractive pools there was no sign of a run of fish except a rather sparse run of humpbacks. There was a fair number of pre-migrant steelheads in the upper pools.

This rather slender evidence strongly suggests that my friend had found an atypical summer steelhead run, one that enters the river in June and July, spawns almost immediately and returns promptly to salt water after spawning; from the rather small size of the fish, it would seem also that their salt-water migration may be limited. Alternatively it is possible that the fish had passed on to pools higher up the river than we were able to go, but I do not think this is altogether likely. A spawning run of this type reflects in some degree the run of May fish in the Campbell and, even more closely, the July spawning fish of Coal Creek. Conditions at Moyeha, which heads in an area of unusually high rainfall, may have forced development of a run of summer spawners rather than a run that holds over through the winter to spawn in the following April.

At this point it is worth recalling the probable development of the steelhead from its common progenitor with the Atlantic salmon since the time about a million years ago when the arctic ice barriers effectively separated the Atlantic and Pacific Oceans. In that massive period of time the North Pacific Ocean has suffered many impressive geological and climatic changes. The steelhead has persisted through them all. Many stocks must have been entirely wiped out by volcanic action; periodic ice ages must have forced southward retreats more than once. Yet today steelhead runs are present in the great majority of streams that flow into the north temperate zone of the Pacific Ocean. This persistence and wide distribution argues repeated and rapid reoccupation of spawning waters as they became livable after each succeeding natural cataclysm, and this in turn suggests a rather wide range of habit that permitted prompt adaptation to any conditions that were reasonably favorable. One of the most important factors most certainly has been this constant presence of small atypical spawning stocks and another is the wide range of fresh-water tolerance, from almost a full year between entry and spawning to almost immediate spawning after entry. Variations such as these mean, and must always have meant, that some part of a stock is always ready to take fullest advantage of the conditions and multiply accordingly.

How long it will take to sort out and recognize all the different types of steelhead runs, apart from the orthodox summer and winter runs, I do not know, but at the present rate of progress it will be a very long while. In the meantime discovery and exploration of what seem to be new summer steelhead streams will continue to be puzzling and difficult and sometimes frustrating, but always intensely interesting. The possible reward, after all, is very great— nothing less than some of the finest fly-fishing in the world.

2. *Steelhead and the Dry Fly — Further Notes*

IN *Fisherman's Summer* I DESCRIBED IN some detail the successful use of a floating fly for summer steelhead. Since that time I have had many opportunities to test the matter further, especially in the Heber River, and I am more than ever convinced that dry-fly fishing, under summer and fall conditions, is the most effective fly-fishing method, as well as the most attractive.

The Heber is a beautiful little stream that flows down the westward slope of Vancouver Island to join the Gold River about eight miles above salt water. It is purely a mountain stream, originating in two deep transverse valleys just over the divide. The stream from the first of these valleys, Crest Creek, has now been permanently diverted for power purposes—an act of vandalism that certainly rates high among the criminal abuses of natural resources. Part of the Heber's flow, from the second valley, is also diverted, but at least this is a controlled diversion and the water can be left to find its proper channel when needed. The normal flow from the Heber valley is not great, but a few miles farther down it is joined by another substantial creek and from there on takes its true form. Like most mountain streams, the Heber can rise seven or eight feet overnight and becomes a raging torrent, unapproachable and unfishable between its rock and timbered walls. But at normal flow it is a beautifully clear, slightly greenish flow among great round boulders and through deep quiet pools. One can wade across it at several places without difficulty but not without feeling the pull of its powerful currents. A mile or more of deep canyon is inaccessible so far as I know—in places the walls on both sides are precipitous and over two hundred feet high. Outside the canyon stretches there are a dozen or so deep pools, nearly all of which hold fish when the run is in. The approach to the stream is nearly everywhere steep, so that one can look down into the pools from a distance and study the fish before going down to the water.

At the ordinary summer and fall levels of July, August and September the fish collect in the deep pools and hold there. They are quite nervous in the low water, and one fish disturbed from the head or the tail of the pool spreads alarm through them all. Once they are alarmed it is very hard to move them to a fly, wet or dry, and almost as difficult to persuade them with a lure of any kind, though one will sooner or later strike at a cherry-bobber or spin-and-glow or something of that sort if it is hung among them near bottom. Bait, especially fresh salmon roe, is another matter. I have seen four fish taken from one pool in quick succession by a roe fisherman standing in plain sight on the bank. Fortunately few bait fishermen have so far found their way to the Heber.

Occasionally one finds a fish alone in streamy water near the head of a pool or alone in some minor pool among the boulders. In either case an accurate cast from downstream with a good floating fly on a No. 8 hook is almost certain to bring a faithful head and tail rise. This is easy fishing, but it does not happen too often. If the water is high enough to make a fairly good flow right through the pools, a wet fly fished downstream may do well; either the ordinary wet-fly or greased-line techniques will take fish in normal water if the fisherman is able to keep out of sight and work his fly down to or over the fish without much disturbance. But in normal or low-summer and fall water the upstream dry fly offers very real advantages, as well as the most exciting and satisfying form of fishing it is possible to imagine.

The best holding pools on the Heber start about a mile above its junction with the Gold and continue from there in a series to the mouth of the main canyon; above the canyon there are several other holding pools below the falls, which seem to block the fish at all stages of water. On one of my first visits to the stream I explored the lower canyon, which is extremely narrow, with very deep pools, expecting to find fish there even though I might not be able to catch them. I found a few good cutthroats, but no steelhead at all, so I turned downstream to explore the junction. Between this lower canyon and the Gold there is a long straight rapid with no holding water, but at the junction the powerful flood waters of the Heber have dug a deep semicircular pool into the bed of the Gold, with

more eddies and conflicting currents than a wise fisherman would choose to fish in a lifetime. But the Heber
was extremely low and it seemed to me that the pool was
a logical place for fish to hold and wait for better water,
so I went to work as best I could and threw my fly out
over the depths. In time I sorted out some of the currents
and eddies and even began to feel quite pleased with my
fishing, but nothing paid the slightest attention to my fly.

The flow of the Heber was coming out from among its
boulders in three swift white runs, so I turned my attention to these. I did not expect much of the first, because
it was the smallest, but I danced my fly down it several
times and nothing happened. The middle run was a little
more impressive, but I could move nothing in it nor in the
smooth water between the runs. The third run, under the
far bank, was the most substantial of the three, very fast
and broken as it came from the rapid, but spreading quickly
as it came over the deep water of the pool. I threw well
up just into the near edge of it. The fly floated beautifully for a fraction of a second, then two perfectly good
steelhead came out at it together. I found time to consider
the misfortune that had put the two of them there and
undoubtedly ensured that both would miss the fly, but
even in the moment of the thought I was sure that the
larger of the two fish had the fly. I felt her solidly as I
tightened, and a moment later she was running directly
towards me. Even then I had only limited faith in the situation, but the hook hold was good and she took no advantage of the big river, fighting a slow, deep, strong but never
violent fight within the limits of the pool. Before the end
I had good reason to be sorry the fight was not more

violent; my little eight-foot rod would lift her to the surface again and again where a powerful swirl of her tail would force me to release line and let her run back for the depths. But in the end I beached a fine clean six-pound fish.

In the closing stages a second still larger fish had been following my hooked fish, which I felt confirmed my idea that a good number of Heber fish were waiting in the pool, so I turned back to the run at the mouth of the stream with full confidence. The second fish that had risen with the other should certainly be there; behind him, farther down the run, there might well be others. Perhaps they were there but nothing else came to my fly and nothing came to the wet fly that I worked carefully down into the depths of the pool. I was left with the memory of those two fish, clearly seen against the bright water, rising to the same artificial fly, and a firmer conviction than ever that a floating fly is powerfully attractive to summer fish.

Later that day, a few hundred yards up the Gold from the mouth of the Heber, I found another fish that further strengthened my conviction. The river is wide at that point, breaking into a rapid, with a strong run under the far bank that I could just reach by wading deeply and casting all the line I could. A fair-sized fish rose to the fly on its first drift and was hooked long enough to take a few yards of line off the reel when the fly came free. I recovered and cast again. The fly was taken down at about the same point by what I thought was the same fish. This time he ran almost to the rapid, where the fly came away. There was a lot of line out and I began to retrieve it slowly, in disgust. To my astonishment, I saw that the fish was following the fly. He came at it and missed, but I could still see him so I continued my slow recovery. He was still following, a few feet behind, so I let the fly drift back, watched him rise to it and turn away, then struck hard. This time he was securely hooked. He was a small male steelhead, not much over two pounds, with milts in about the same stage of early development as the ovaries of the fish I had killed at the mouth of the Heber. In his stomach were five large winged dragonflies, which may explain his determination to attack my fly. Dragonflies can bite, and it seems possible that each prick of my hook simply strengthened his idea that he had found another of these fine, satisfying creatures.

A fish of this size, at this stage of maturity, is rather hard to place. Presumably it is a precocious male returning to spawn after a very short stay in the sea, and as such it would be more foolish and more aggressive than most full-grown steelheads. I have found dragonfly nymphs in the stomachs of full-grown steelhead but never that I can recall a winged dragonfly. I have seen a winged dragonfly flutter and struggle across the surface of a pool over the heads of a dozen steelhead without being taken, yet I have no doubt they are taken at times, as are most other things, from duck feathers to drifting salmon eggs, from bees and sedges to stone-fly nymphs and caddis grubs. The steelhead is not a very discriminating fish, but he is extremely capricious. It is well to work on the probabilities, such as a properly drifted fly that suggests a half-drowned bee or yellow jacket or deer fly, but if these fail it may be well to see what happens to a skated spider or a sodden fly dragging clumsily across the surface.

There were other fish and other incidents on that sunny September day, but only one that still seems significant. Though I am not above caching a couple of bottles of beer in the creek on a hot day, I learned long ago to drink water sparingly in the woods. That particular year was 1958, the centennial year of the province of British Columbia, and to do it honor I had grown a handsome beard and a massive, well-tended mustache. Shortly after the dragonfly-chasing fish had insisted on committing suicide, I realized I was thirsty. A small bright creek came murmuring off the hill nearby, so I turned to it and drank, putting my face to the water. Even as I drank I realized that the heavy mustache was giving a new dimension to what is always a simple act of intense pleasure. As I stood up the pleasure was repeated and intensified. There was a fresh coolness on the upper lip, then, a moment later, a trickle of coolness across both lips as drops of water drained down from the heavy growth above. Perhaps this has nothing to do with fishing, but my beardless lips remember it as clearly as my eyes remember the double rise to the single fly or the determined chase of the dragonfly specialist.

3. *An Ideal Stream*

ON LARGE, FAST WATER STREAMS WITH sparse runs of summer fish, experiment is slow and difficult. One rarely sees a fish until he rises and then only briefly. What has happened immediately before, what happens after are largely matters of interpretation and guesswork. Much of the time one is searching over wide reaches of water without the slightest knowledge of whether fish are there or not or, if they are there, where they are. The Heber, with its deep, clear, smooth-surfaced pools, is entirely another matter, especially in low water. One sees almost everything and learns what to expect quite rapidly.

Fishing Heber Creek I generally use an eight-foot cane rod weighing about four ounces, with an HCH or HCF fly line, a hundred yards of backing and leaders tapered to 1x—sometimes to 3x. Most of my fish have been taken on a No. 8 hook with a dressing I now call the Steelhead Bee. The dressing is as follows:

Tail: Fox squirrel. Slightly longer than hook shank.

Body: Dark brown floss silk divided by single bar of
yellow silk, making three equal bars, brown, yellow
brown.

Hackle: Natural red, sparse.

Wings: Fox squirrel, set slightly forward and well
divided. These also should be slightly longer than
the hook shank and, like the tail, fairly bushy.

There is nothing sacred or mystic about this dressing,
except perhaps its general shape and coloration. Other
brown hairs than fox squirrel may be used and I have often
used them. The body may be made of fur dubbing instead
of silk, and the hackle could equally well be ginger or
honey. In heavy water a No. 6 hook is not too large; in
very low water No. 10 or even No. 12 may be a little
better. But after using the fly in various forms for more
than ten years I feel that if a steelhead can be persuaded
to rise to the surface at all he will come to this pattern
just as surely as any other.

This tackle is, I believe, nicely calculated to the size of
the fish and of the river. The fish have lost the impetuosity
of salt water and are fairly easily followed if they leave
the pools. The rod may be a little short occasionally, when
a long cast is needed or in steering the line around rocks,
but its shortness is an advantage in approaching the fish
from behind. The 3x leader is a mixture of propitiation,
vanity and laziness—laziness when I don't bother to change
after using a spider, vanity because it is nice to feel one is
handling a six-pound fish on 3x, propitiation when I turn
to it with the feeling that I will risk anything to stir some

stubborn fish. But I suspect that it is rarely if ever needed with the No. 8 fly.

Partly because the water where one finds them is generally quite smooth and partly because they have had time to forget their desperate wildness and shyness, the Heber fish usually rise quite slowly and deliberately. My friend Wilf Hill once watched a fish rise to my fly in the tiny pool immediately above the Iron Gate Pool and described it carefully to me later.

The pool is just below a little fall where the water foams out over smooth pale rock to break on a great brown boulder and turn into a rippled glide close under a twenty-foot bluff. The glide is perhaps six or seven feet deep at low water, and the whole pool is not much over eighty feet long. The fish, if there is one there, usually lies on the edge of the glide, a few feet below the boulder and a few feet out from the bluff.

Wilf signaled from the top of the bluff as soon as I entered the lower end of the pool that the fish was there. I fished my way slowly and carefully up the glide, in case there was another fish he had not seen and also to be sure that everything was working properly before I came to the critical cast. After some half-dozen casts I knew I was in position, drew a little line off the reel and set the fly just above where the fish should be. Almost as it landed I heard Wilf yell, glanced up at him then quickly back to my fly. It had disappeared and the rings of the calm rise were already widening across the glide. I raised the rod and set the hook solidly. The timing was perfect.

The fish was a clean, bright, five-pound female just over twenty-four inches long. Wilf said she had been lying near bottom until the fly landed. She let it drift just past her, then moved to it very slowly, dropping back, mouth open, turning up, then rolling forward to take it. The whole movement, he said, was like a vertical "S" curve, timed perfectly to intercept the fly and take it down.

I have not yet been able to observe another rise so clearly and accurately, but my impression is that a fish usually does drop back a little way under a normally drifting fly, then curve upwards and forwards to meet it. No one could ask for much more than this, and it makes the best possible case for offering a smooth, orthodox drift before attempting to tease fish up with a dragged or skated fly.

One of the most interesting and varied days I have spent on the Heber was in early August a year ago with Skate Hames, a frequent fishing companion, and Cleve Grant, the lecturer and wildlife photographer. The main purpose was to get some pictures for Cleve, of the stream and its fish, of the dry fly and its possibilities, though Skate brought along his wet-fly rod and a sinking line as a check on the other.

The first pool we stopped at was the Stump Pool, so called because one stands by a stump on the right bank, some thirty feet above the water, to look down into the pool. There were four or five good fish holding lazily about halfway down the pool, fairly well over towards the rock face below us, where the water was eight or ten feet deep. The river was low, at least six inches lower than good fishing height, and the morning was sunny, with only occasional clouds. The pool is right beside the road and is fished fairly often, so Skate did not think too much of our chances, but I am always optimistic when I can see fish, so Cleve and I crossed well below the pool and I began to fish it from the tail.

Even when all the fish seem to be well up in the body of a pool, it is important to start at the tail and work up. I kept well down, using a backhand cast with the rod almost horizontal, covering the edge of the pool's gliding current first, then the center of it, then reaching over to let the fly drift along close to the rock face. Skate signaled that the fish were still holding and seemed undisturbed. I set the fly over towards the rock face again, still some feet below where the fish were lying, and it disappeared at once in a nice quiet rise. The fish ran hard upstream and jumped beautifully, and I hoped Cleve had the camera on her.

This was a small fish, rather under four pounds, and Skate said later that she was not one of those we had seen originally, but had come from somewhere out of sight, close under the rock face. I fished on over the other fish but could not rise them, which was not surprising as the pool had been a good deal disturbed. Close under the rapids at the head, in the eddy between two strong runs, I rose a fish of about six pounds, but did not hook him. It was a wild, quick rise and I supposed he was one of the fish I had disturbed in the lower part of the pool.

The next two pools were disappointing. Skate's favorite, where the stream divides around an island, was too low— there was no flow at all behind the island—and held no fish. The next pool above is large and slow and deep, with its main flow curving around a rock outcrop near the head. We spotted a fish well down the pool, but while we watched he suddenly swam hard for the head and disappeared. I suppose he may have seen us, though we were standing quite well back and in the shadow of the timber. In any case, we took no more chances. Cleve and I crossed over below the tail and I fished up carefully, all the way to the head. The first cast into the near run was taken by a yearling. The next cast, to the center run, bounced down without a touch. The third run was the heaviest and I felt some confidence I could find the fish there, but again the fly bounced down untouched. I dropped a cast into the smooth water between the runs and the fish came to it immediately, from the direction of the heavy run, almost straight towards me. He swirled violently at the fly, drew it under and turned back for the run; I struck and felt nothing at all. The movement was much too fast for certainty, yet I was certain he had missed the fly and simply drowned it with the violence of his break. He would not come again, though I suspect he might have come back to the drowned fly if I had left it there.

There were heavier clouds around now, so we decided to go on to the Iron Gate Pool, which lies out in the logging slash, and work up to the pools in the timber later. The Iron Gate Pool is beautiful holding water. The current flows in at the head around a great jutting shoulder of bare rock, smooths out in the throat over six feet or more of water and spreads from there fairly evenly through the pool, leaving an eddy on either side at low water but gathering again to a sweeping flow over the wide tail. One comes to the pool down a steep slope and usually stops eighty to a hundred feet above the water to spot the fish. We did so on this day, and found them.

The water was glassy green and smooth as silk over the

body of the pool. The rocks of the bottom are very large, brown and gray and white. There is a huge flat white rock in the throat of the pool, just below the jutting shoulder, and several fish showed intermittently over it in the strong current. But there were also fish scattered through the rest of the pool, a dozen or more of them, moving calmly and lazily, one or two of them working right down into the tail. The fish in the current at the throat of the pool would have been easy to take on a floating fly—if one could have approached them. To approach from below would have meant disturbing the other fish and almost certainly transmitting their nervousness to the fish in the throat. To drift a fly down from above would be to hook one fish and disturb the whole pool for him.

Skate said: "It doesn't look too easy. How are we going to do it?"

Sitting there on the bluff and watching them, I felt as I always do that I could take every fish in the pool—and perhaps I could, if each could be isolated from all the others. But I managed to be cautious. "I think I can work up from below without disturbing them too much," I said. "Then you can get behind the shoulder and work a wet fly down to the ones in the throat."

At low water there is a nice gravel bar along the right side of the pool from which one can reach nearly everything, from the tail almost to the throat. Cleve and I went down to it while Skate watched from the hillside. Out of respect for the clear water and the glassy smoothness of the pool I tied on a 3x leader and my finest honey spider on a No. 14 hook. Even from where we were, almost on a

level with the water, I could see many of the fish and I
looked the pool over carefully to make sure none was
below me before I ventured out on to the gravel bar. I
crept out and knelt at the edge. I had released my fly and
begun to let out line when I saw a fish swimming slowly
upstream from below me. I froze and let him pass, pray-
ing that he was the only one, wondering if the damage was
already done. He held on his unhurried way and disappeared into the deep water.

I began fishing, using a horizontal sidearm cast, allowing the feathery air resistance of the spider to hold it back
so that the leader curved upstream and let the fly come first
over the fish. I was very careful, throwing only about forty
feet of line straight upstream, lengthening five or six feet
more on the next cast, towards midstream, then a little more
to reach straight across, letting the fly drift past me before
each recovery. As the current creases changed on the
surface I could see the shapes of fish below. I knew that
nearly every cast was covering them and I knew that they
were paying no attention at all, even before Skate signaled
to that effect from his high post.

I have taken more than one good summer steelhead on
a drifted spider and I was ready for a rise at every cast,
but my real hope at this time was to get the fish used to
me and my movements without frightening them and perhaps to interest them in the surface by the repeated drift
of the fly. They began to show interest. First one, then
another turned downstream as the fly passed, circled under
it and moved back up. Skate signaled the change and convinced me that my hopes were not deceiving me. One fish
in particular, towards midstream, circled back under every
drift that passed over him.

There was a heavy cloud overhead now and a few drops of rain fell on the smooth surface of the pool. I cut off the spider and tied on the No. 8 Steelhead Bee I had been using before. By this time I had moved halfway up along the bar and there were fish opposite me, even downstream of me, as well as upstream, but there was no sign of panic or alarm in them.

My first cast with the new fly was almost straight upstream, on the edge of the current. A fish rose perfectly within the first foot or so of the drift. I struck him solidly. He ran hard upstream, jumped splendidly, straight out, ran on from the jump, and the fly came away. Behind me Cleve's camera was working, but I was disappointed.

By this time it was raining quite heavily, big drops that splashed on the pool and broke its surface. I dried off my fly and went on casting. Nothing moved to the first drift, nor to the second, which I had placed about midstream. The third drift was well over and I had to let the fly sweep across below me, dragging slightly. A fish came to it right on the surface, mouth wide open and straight towards me. I let him have it, gave him time to turn and struck, none too hopefully. He was well hooked and fought hard. One run was upstream and across almost to the head of the pool, where he jumped far out with the line completely drowned, but the 3x leader held. I finally beached a really bright fresh fish of four and a half pounds.

We ate lunch and rested the pool, then Skate went upstream above the rock shoulder and worked a Money Special well down among the fish in the throat. He hooked a strong fish almost immediately and had to come down over the rock with it. The fish fought hard, running and jumping with real power, but it stayed in the pool and he

beached it on the gravel bar—a female, twenty-nine inches
long and nine and a half pounds, the biggest fish either of
us had taken from the Heber so far.

We rested the pool again, briefly, but the fish were still
nervous when I waded in above the gravel bar to try for
three that were still passing back and forth over the white
rock in the throat. A fish rose to about the sixth cast, taking
the fly rather violently. He turned at once, ran straight
downstream, jumped and the fly came away. After that
nothing else in the pool would come to wet fly or dry.

This describes a fairly typical low-water day on a really
good summer steelhead stream. By Frederick Halford's
standards for the chalk streams, it would have to be considered a rather untidy and unorthodox occasion, but I
find it difficult to imagine fishing of any kind that would
be more exciting, more interesting or more satisfying. That
only two fish were killed out of six risen to the floating
fly is unusual. It is even more unusual, in my experience,
that two of the four fish lost should have thrown the fly
after rising to a straight drift on an upstream cast, while
one of the fish killed was securely hooked on a dragging
fly that had been carried downstream of the rod. But the
record is balanced somewhat by the fact that two, if not
three, of the fish that were missed or lost had been disturbed before rising.

It is worth asking whether the wet fly might not have
produced better results. As the day went and the fish lay,
I do not think it could possibly have risen even half as
many fish because of the inevitable disturbance of the
pools; an upstream nymph or an upstream greased-line
technique, skillfully handled, might have done as well,

but I think it is unlikely and neither could have given the same visual pleasures and satisfactions. Any competent bait fisherman could have taken as many fish as we hooked, and more besides, with a fraction of the effort; but I doubt if that has any bearing on the matter. A drag seine would have done quite well, too.

I visited the Heber again three or four weeks later with Martin Bovey. There had been little or no rain in the meanwhile and the stream had dropped ten or twelve inches, to a lower level than I had ever seen before. Even so, there were fish in the pools and I thought at first it would be possible to catch them. But the flow was so feeble that they were facing in every direction—upstream, downstream, across and at various angles, presumably finding little vagaries of current that comforted them. A few fish were holding in the throat of the Iron Gate Pool and two or three in the pool above. But every approach was met squarely by the cold, appraising stare of two or three other fish and every movement on the bank stirred unhappy movement in the pool. I tried nymphs, even weighted nymphs; but we moved nothing and hooked nothing. Had we found a fish alone in lively water, I think he might have come to the fly, but the fish were collected in the deeper pools and favorable spots like the tiny pool above the Iron Gate Pool held nothing at all.

Now that access to the Heber has become relatively easy, I am not sure how long its good fishing will last. The stream has no protective regulations—any season is open season, any bait or lure is legal. Under low-water conditions such as I have just described, there is nothing to prevent the snagger going to work if bait will not take fish for him—and he will go to work. The stream's natural protections are its canyon reaches and, in most places, the steep slopes above its banks. I am almost certain that it has no significant winter run, yet fish are taken there all through the winter.

First-class fishing can only be maintained in a small accessible stream of this kind by intelligent regulation. The Heber should be closed to all fishing from October thirty-first to May fifteenth each year; pre-migrant steelhead should be protected by a fourteen-inch size limit; fishing should be limited to the unweighted fly only, wet or dry; water from the Crest Creek diversion should be returned to its normal channel and the Heber diversion should be closely regulated; possibly a fish pass should be installed at the falls to open up good spawning water in the upper reaches.

None of these things will be done until too late. In the meanwhile one can hope for a few more years of good fishing, then a decline until the bait fisher and the snagger are discouraged by the law of diminishing returns and the stream comes back to the fly-fisher again. After that there may be proper regulation and perhaps some extravagant attempts to restore the run. But runs are much more easily maintained than restored—especially runs of fish that are as little understood as the summer steelhead.

4. *More Fast-Water Rises*

I HAVE SUGGESTED THAT STEELHEAD RISE A good deal more readily in fast, streamy water than in smooth water. But I am afraid it is equally true that one is considerably less likely to hook the fish that rises in fast water, especially if he weighs less than five or six pounds.

I have suggested also that this is to be expected of cutthroat trout and rainbows, which often rise from the bottom rather than from a position just under the surface like brown trout. It is also to be expected of sea-run fish that are not used to river feeding and river currents. We are inclined to think that a fish can do just about anything he likes in the water and, compared to a man, he can. But his body is subject to the same laws of current flow and current whimsy as is a man's, even though in less degree. Even though his reactions are five times as fast as those of a man, his eyes can still be deceived by broken light and erratic action. The resident trout is dealing with these

things every day, of course, and learns to do very well
with them—but even Ted Williams has been known to
take a strike or pop up an infield fly. The sea-run fish is
like a ball player at the first batting practice of the season,
liable to be quite a bit off his timing; and to make matters
even worse, he is not normally a hungry player.

Fast-water rises remain fascinating to me, in spite of all
the explanations I can think up for them, because they are
so often spectacular and beautiful and they are invariably
exciting. Thoughts of solving them or of markedly increasing my percentage of hooked fish are no longer much
in my mind, but I doubt if I shall ever tire of stirring fish
to the surface through fast water or if my enjoyment is
significantly less for the fish I miss or that miss my fly.

One sunny mid-September day a year or two ago, with
the river very low, I was able to wade upstream behind
the big rock in the Line Fence Pool and drift a fly re-
peatedy over the fast water beyond it. My real purpose
was to see if I could find a stray summer steelhead in what
I know to be a good winter lie. It was soon clear that there
was nothing around of any size, but there was a wonderful
assortment of steelhead pre-migrants and small rainbows
running from six to twelve inches scattered through the
heavy water and they put on a fine demonstration of fast-
water rises. The water over which I was floating my fly
is for the most part not over four or five feet deep, flowing
at around three or four miles an hour, its surface rippled
and broken by passage over the rocky bottom.

The sun was at just the right angle to show me the little
fish perfectly as they moved up to the fly, and the fly
rode well and showed up well. In spite of the size of the

fly—it was a No. 6 or No. 8 hook, I am not sure which—
and the speed of the flow, most of the rises were extraordi-
narily accurate. Time and again fish of six or eight inches
met the fly perfectly and took it smoothly down with head
and tail rises. A few rises missed the fly altogether, but
such misses were usually followed by a quick, fierce chase
and a successful rise; one or two fish were fast enough to
make several attempts and recoveries within a few feet
of drift. A good proportion of the rises were follow-backs,
downstream rushes close under the surface that ended in
swirling and usually successful rises. I was not striking at
all, but in thirty or forty rises that took the fly down I
only had to release two fish; one or two others were
briefly hooked and got rid of the fly on their own. The
speed of rejection was quite remarkable, because the pull
of the line in the current would have set the hook very
quickly even without a strike.

One cannot draw many useful conclusions from the
actions of small fish like this; big fish are slower and more
deliberate, less flexible in movement, more powerful against
a strong current. But it seems unlikely that their vision
differs greatly from that of smaller fish. I tried to detect
some pattern of performance in the varying rises. It was
clear, for instance, that most, though not all, the head and
tail rises came to the fly when it was drifting freely, without drag; most of the follow-backs came to a dragging fly,
though again this was not always true. The misses seemed
to be about equally divided between free drift and drag.
All the fish seemed to be coming up from a considerable
depth, probably from the bottom. The only firm conclusion I reached was that both the type and the efficiency

of the rise depended on how and when the fish saw the
fly. The dancing, broken mirror of the undersurface would
now reveal it, now obscure it almost entirely by chance
and the fish, holding down near bottom, swayed and tossed
in the varying flow among the rocks, were reacting to
momentary glimpses of it rather than plain sight. Since
that time, with face mask and diving suit, precariously
gripping the rocks, I have been down on that same bottom
among the fish and I am more than ever convinced that
this is so.

I can think of no reason to believe that larger fish would
see more effectively; their greater strength might allow
them to respond a little more accurately, but their more
deliberate movements would make the responses less frequent. Certainly I have seen every type of rise that the
little fish revealed to me that day exactly reproduced by
very much larger fish.

I went over most of this in my mind while I was there,
but it was not why I stayed so long. I stayed because it
was so beautiful. The water with the strong sun forcing
through it had the quality of great masses of transparent,
fluid silk. The little fish were enclosed in it, embraced by
it, comfortable and sure, supported, upheld, possessed.
Their shapes were suddenly visible as they rose from the
bottom, ideal and complete, invisible again almost as they
became visible, yet leaving a sharp and perfect impression on the mind's eye. Some had brown backs in the sunlight, some greenish, some steel-gray; some flashed silvery
bellies in turning to the fly, some flicked their tails out, a
few raised glistening backs through the surface film. One
or two jumped right out and came down on the fly. They
were a succession of brilliant impressions, brightly remem-

bered and beloved. A big fish, had one been there, might have left a stronger and more lasting impression as he came to the fly, but his single magnificence would not have equaled the lively repetitions of the little fish.

At about this time I did rise a fair-sized fish in fast water whose image remains clear and constant in my mind. Again it was in bright sunlight, but this time at the tail of the Lower Island Pool. The river was rather high, so I had started well down, casting a long line up towards the bar. For some reason I had put up a beautifully hackled No. 14 iron-blue spider on a 3x leader. I rose a fish of about twelve inches and carefully gave him time to get rid of the fly. Moving from him changed the angle of the sun so that I seemed to be looking almost horizontally into the two or three feet of water where my fly would next land. I made the cast, saw the fly land perfectly, sitting high on its long hackles. Then I saw the fish, rising up through the sunny water, very slowly and easily. I even saw the slight thrust of his tail as he moved to complete the interception. He was a male steelhead of three and a half pounds, rather slender, a little dark. He ran from his rise, hard downstream, and jumped at the head of the rapid. When I persuaded him back from this he ran again upstream and across, forty yards into the backing. In the end I had to go down to the lower pool with him and the landing net collapsed on my first try, though I was able to flip it over and bring him back to it. If he had been a fresh fish I think he would have broken me—perhaps much earlier on in the proceeding.

This I would judge to be one of the rarer fast-water rises, to a fly perfectly seen through several feet of its drift, probably because the surface of the water was comparatively smooth, possibly because of the angle of the sun. The

fly, with its fine, dry hackles, can have made only the
slightest impression on the surface of the water, yet the fish
was aware of it when it was still three or four feet upstream
and he was able to meet it with only the slightest adjustment of his horizontal position in the water. Perhaps I am
wrong in considering it a fast-water rise at all under these
special circumstances, yet it is a rise that can occur in fast-
water slicks and the fast-water fisherman should be aware
of it.

The next rise that comes readily to my mind is not so
memorable for the rise itself as for its demonstration of a
fast-water principle—that rainbows and cutthroats tend to
run away to deeper water from a missed rise. I had been up
along the far side of the river to the Power House Pool
and had done fairly well there, though by no means well
enough to counteract my irritation over the awkward and
uncomfortable fishing or my regret for the superb pool it
had once been. On the way back I turned in at the Lower
Island Pool, which is another good spot to fray a temper
under the present conditions of almost constant high flow.
What was once a gravel bar is now under eighteen inches
of water, though it still splits the flow, forcing a really fast
run under the cut bank and leaving a race of wild water
through the main channel along the outside edge of the bar.

The run under the cut bank is not much over three or
four feet wide, but it is fully four feet deep through much
of its length and five or six feet at its deepest part. I have
taken a few fish of two pounds or better from this run
since the river was high in the fall months and so always
make a few casts into it before working down the main
pool. The first cast on this occasion produced a fierce and
massive swirl that took the fly down, though I felt no resist-

ance to the strike. He would not come again for the floating fly, nor for the wet, so I decided to fish on down the
main pool with the wet fly and come back to him again
with a new floater.

The main pool is not especially awkward to fish, except
for the very fast current, but the fish are nearly always
right down at the tail and a fish of any size is bound to go
out. One has to follow into water that is almost over one's
waders, under the limbs of a spruce, a cedar and an alder
whose overhang actually touches the surfaces in places. One
can occasionally turn and bring back a two-pounder; one
follows a four-pounder with some confidence, but anything
much larger than that is likely to pass beyond recovery and
beyond following into the rapid below while one is nego-
tiating the tree limbs.

It happened on this occasion that I moved nothing in the
main pool, so I turned back to look for the fish under the
bank with some determination. In spite of the impressive
swirl of his rise, I guessed that he was not much over two
pounds; but even so, I could see some good reasons why I
might not land him if I hooked him, chief among them a
dead alder that had fallen head first down the cut bank
and was angled right across the run. I thought of going in
to pull it out of there, but decided the risk of disturbing
the fish was too great. I put on a new 2x leader and one of
my best Steelhead Bees on a No. 6 hook and began to fish
my way up the run. I searched carefully and thoroughly,
right up to the place where the fish had first risen, and
nothing moved to the fly. It seemed to me that any fish
lying anywhere within the run must certainly have seen the
fly. I had been keeping well back on the drowned gravel
bar and felt that my search would have disturbed nothing,

so I moved down and started up again. The water was greenest and deepest right up against the cut bank, dancing along its conglomerate surface well under the shade of the overhanging alders.

This time, partly to entertain myself, I tried to set every second cast tight against the cut bank, so that the fly in its drift scraped along the protruding cobbles of its face. There, two or three yards below where it had first risen and from what must have been precisely the deepest place in the whole run, the fish came up very fast and took the fly down cleanly.

There was trouble, of course: trouble with the dead alder, trouble under the spruce limbs, where the bright silvery fish chose to jump several times in rapid succession, trouble in the current of the main stream, trouble where the current breaks fast at the tail of the bar, more trouble with the dead alder on the way back. Through it all, to the very last moments, I remained convinced that I had a fish of not much over two pounds and treated it accordingly, refusing to follow down, turning it out of the currents by deliberate force, finally walking it back upstream on a tight line. It was only as I brought it over the net that I realized the extent of my audacity. It was a magnificent fresh-run cutthroat female, twenty-two inches long and just under four pounds. In the opposite side of her jaw from my fly there was a worm fisherman's hook on a short ten-pound breaking-strain leader; the leader had held, but the six-pound breaking-strain line it was attached to had not.

If I read too much into an incident like this, it is simply through the inevitable weakness of the angler's position— he must observe and interpret as best he can from above the surface of the water; much of the charm and nearly all the mystery of the sport is in this. But the reading here seems unusually clear. The fish was lying well up in the ideal feeding station, in the comparatively shallow water at the head of the run, when it first swirled at the fly. Frightened by its own boldness, it fled at once to the deepest, most sheltered spot in the run and was possibly held there still more firmly by my passage down the gravel bar. As I worked back again, the fly may have been too far out for the fish's range of vision in the fast, broken water or she may have been too nervous to expose herself again over the lighter and shallower water; experience with the worm hook, echoed by the missed rise, may well have been a further influence. But when the fly came directly over, under the very shadow of the cut bank, she not only saw it plainly but could rise to it without risk of exposing herself unduly.

The question that follows immediately upon such supported speculation as this is: how best to put it to use? Often one is merely confirmed in a practice that has already proved effective. I began using the large hair-wing dry flies in fast water because they floated so well. Later I realized that they moved fish better than well-hackled flies that sat higher in the water and decided that this was because they looked like some large terrestrial creature struggling to hold its place on the surface film—bee, ant, wasp, termite or deer fly. I suspect now that the real reason may be simply that they are more easily seen by the fish in the shifting, broken, mirror undersurface of fast water.

My first reason for using deliberate drag on a dry fly in fast water was that accidental drag had sometimes risen fish for me. I decided then that it was a logical as well as a pragmatic decision because many winged creatures do move on the surface of the water. I still believe this to be so, but I suspect it is also true that the dragging fly is more easily seen by the fish under the adverse conditions of fast water.

Years ago, when I began to make a habit of searching for steelhead in fast water, I often spent a great deal of time trying to move a fish that had already risen to my fly and missed or been missed. In time I learned that the best thing to do was to try another three or four casts to the same spot, move on and come back later. I still think that the best chance of rising the fish again is to leave him for an hour or so, but before doing so I make casts to three different spots; first, to the point where he rose; next, well upstream along the line of the fly's float, in case he has drifted back under it or followed back behind it; and thirdly to the nearest likely hiding place, which is often indicated by a glimpse of the fish's movement away from his unsuccessful rise. If none of the three ventures is successful within two or three drifts, I move on and come back later if I can.

Every so often one or another of these intelligent explorations pays off; the fish rises and I feel that I am really growing in understanding of fish and their ways. More often nothing happens at all and I am left still floundering in my ignorance. The laughing water dances on over the sunny shallows and into the greener depths, revealing nothing at all. I comfort myself then with the thought that what we fishermen attain from our position above the surface is not so much knowledge as a different degree of ignorance—which is not without its special satisfactions in a day when most specialists know so much.

PART FIVE
Aquarium Notes

1. *Acquisition*

ONE MORNING AT BREAKFAST SOME TWO years ago I saw an advertisement for "complete aquarium kits" at what seemed a remarkably low price. In an unguarded moment I showed it my wife. "That's something I should have done years ago," I said.

"What?" she asked.

"Get one of those things."

"What on earth for?"

"To watch things."

"Goldfish, you mean?" she asked. "What do you care about goldfish?"

"No, no," I said impatiently. "Things from the creeks and the river. Anything and everything. You could set up a whole natural ecology and keep track of it."

"Do you really think you could?"

I admitted I wasn't sure, but failed to add that I hadn't the slightest intention of trying. It was just one of those many things that one really ought to do if there weren't so many other things to do—things that sound fine in the distant talking stage, but would probably seem far less simple if one were actually faced with them. I wasn't faced with this and promptly forgot the idea, as I had several times before.

One morning about a month later—Christmas morning, to be exact—I opened a very large package and uncovered by slow degrees an aquarium set, complete in every detail as the paper had promised—pump, filter, air stone, artificial weeds, china goldfish, instruction book and handsome 20 x 12 x 10 tank. I was, if I may use a phrase that had never before seemed to mean very much, taken aback. "My heavens," I said. "I didn't really mean I *wanted* one."

I was wrong about that and quickly proved it. By mid-afternoon I had covered the bottom of the tank with fine river gravel, set in some cobble-sized rocks, planted some river moss and filled the whole thing with river water. I set up the filter and hooked up the pump, which operated in an offensively noisy way. Then I introduced some caddis larvae and snails, which were the easiest things to catch. This by itself seemed to me and my family a spectacular show. The pump was still noisy and inefficient, so I consulted the instruction book that came with the kit and learned that a real aquarium enthusiast would not expect any sort of efficiency from a pump that did not cost considerably more than the whole elegant outfit. So I took the offending pump apart, played a little with its insides, especially the rubber parts, and put it together again without much hope. Since then it has run silently and efficiently twenty-four hours a day for two years.

My first introductions were cautious and conservative. I tried one or two prickly sculpins, but didn't care much for their large heads and rather aggressive manners, so I settled in the end for two Aleutian sculpins, still bullheads in common language, but somewhat more slender and delicate, with small heads, slate-blue bodies and unspotted dorsal fins. These are bottom dwellers in every British Columbia stream I know, so I felt their introduction was a proper step in setting up an authentic natural habitat, while it would also show whether the aquarium—or I—was capable of keeping fish alive at all.

In everyday life I am not a great admirer of sculpins. They are not the most handsome or impressive of fishes, and I have long been satisfied that they are particularly deadly predators in trout and salmon streams. But it is rather different when you have two of your own.

My sculpins were quite small, the larger about two and a half inches long, the smaller less than two inches. Having no swim bladders, they remained on the bottom most of the time, but every so often they seemed to feel the need of exercise and then they would swim the full length of the tank back and forth in beautiful fading curves that took them almost to the surface and gracefully down again. On the bottom they were extremely alert and efficient, hunting constantly for small caddis or anything else that moved. Their color changes were really impressive. When I first turned them into the tank they were pale, almost sandy, and with little variation from head to tail. I knew that this paleness was a natural reaction of many fish, including trout, to fear or strange surroundings, in large measure a protective reaction. I soon realized it was also a resting

reaction in my bullheads. When hunting or on the aggressive their color darkened through its natural slate-blue
almost to black, and strong white bars showed up. They
hunted with quick movements from place to place, stopping to look for any sign of life on the bottom. If a small
caddis moved in front of them their interest was immediately obvious. Usually they perched up on stiffened ventral
fins that looked like little legs and cocked their heads
downwards or sideways to follow the movement. Often
they adjusted their position two or three times. Then they
pounced upon the unfortunate caddis, stirring up silt from
the bottom in the violence of their movement and running
away from the scene to finish the job of swallowing it.

All this impressed me a good deal when I thought of the
thousands upon thousands of sculpins, like mine and usually
much larger, on every river bottom. I thought of their
effectiveness as defenseless salmon and trout alevins worked
their way up to the surface of the gravel after hatching,
and I felt some gratitude and obligation to the mergansers
who hunt the river bottoms for sculpins through twelve
months of every year. But I did not like my own sculpins
the less for that. They were endearingly bold little creatures and would play like kittens with a small dry fly that
I danced along the outside of the tank. They fed, took
their exercise and rested. Sometimes they perched like little
birds on the weeds, ventral fins stiff, bodies curved for
balance. Above all they lived, and gave me reason to hope
that still more interesting types of fish might survive in my
aquarium and under my clumsy ministrations.

Throughout this cautious two or three months I had a
fairly useful plan in mind. I was curious about the forage

production of Coal Creek over its silted bed, especially the types of creatures that lived in the rather massive growths of hornwort and fountain moss. Remembering the crowded weed beds of the chalk streams, I wondered if these could have taken over the production of the gravel beds. The first step was to replace the river weeds I already had in the aquarium with weeds from Coal Creek. At the same time I began to collect such creatures as I could independently of the weeds; and on all my intermittent visits I kept a close watch for signs of emerging coho fry.

To say that all this was fascinating is a hopeless understatement. I spent hours on end watching the blundering movements of the caddis grubs in search of algae and rotting weed. It was easy to imagine how they became available to trout, especially in swift-flowing streams. Close observation of their cases suggested that exact imitation is a delusion, for the caddis larva is something of an individual. Most of the cases from Coal Creek were circular and made of dark green weed, but other colors were often interwoven with the dark green, entirely at random—now a yellow fragment of frost-killed reed, now the bright new green of fresh growth stood out in vivid contrast to the rest. The sand-grain cases of the river caddis had every conceivable color built into them—gray of granite, white of quartz, rust red of iron, brown and greens and blues. And somewhere on nearly every case was a mirrored grain of mica that caught the light like tinsel—seemingly a perfect touch to catch the eye of a hungry fish. Even the dark cases of rotting wood, some spiraled, some built lengthwise along the body, had distinctive patches of light or dark shading somewhere about them. Generalization is reasonable enough

—gray, brown, dark green—but any fanciful touch the fly-tier cares to throw in is certainly more than justified.

The caddis larvae were easy to observe because my bull-heads could successfully swallow only the smallest of them. May flies were a different matter. In early spring the weeds of Coal Creek held quantities of tiny May-fly larvae of several types, as well as the larger Ephemera and Heptagenia. In the aquarium they excited the bullheads to a frenzy of immediate activity and in no time at all only Ephemera and Heptagenia were left and even those were not safe. I had hoped that one particularly active and beautiful nymph, Callibeatis, would survive, since it reacts quickly and swims very fast. But a single nymph of this species anywhere in the tank stirred the bullheads to relentless determination. They struck, missed, pursued, became lost, hunted again, found again, struck again, missed again, hunted and pursued again until at last they were successful. I tried introducing several nymphs at once in the hope that one or two would escape notice and find security somewhere. Within fifteen minutes all would be gone and the bullheads would be hopping and yawning lazily about on the bottom. For a while I was tempted to get rid of them, but I decided they belonged and left them there.

At about this time I sent away for a small minnow trap which I planned to keep set in the river to pick up whatever it would of nymphs and larvae and small fish. Before it arrived there were free-swimming coho fry in Coal Creek and on April fourth I caught one in a tiny hand net. He was a fine little fish, orange-finned and heavily parr-marked, about one and a half inches long. Neither his capture nor the journey home seemed to bother him, and he even chased a May-fly nymph as I was easing him out of the bucket and into the tank. He settled in at once, holding in mid-water, testing every fragment of drift or movement about him. He picked up many useless things, including reed particles, and spat them out again; to my surprise he even spat out May-fly nymphs at times, though he immediately took them again and swallowed them.

The movements of the bullheads drew his attention from time to time and he investigated them cautiously, but without fear. Occasionally he nipped at a small caddis on the bottom, but apparently they and their cases were too much of an undertaking at his stage of growth because I never saw him swallow one. The small red mites, which seemed to be just his size, he invariably rejected, as did the bullheads. Though he was responsive to nearly all movement, any positive movement straight upward through the water stirred him unfailingly to pursuit and capture. I was more than pleased with him and was carefully calculating how many others I could safely add when I came home one morning to find only the bullheads in the tank. A quick search revealed the little coho on the carpet several feet away, and a few drops of water near the space in the canopy where the air hose led into the tank showed his way of escape to his fate. On April eleventh I went to Coal Creek and picked out three more coho fry from the same place. This time I sealed the space for the air hose with transparent tape.

2. *Observations*

I SEE MANY BEAUTIFUL, GEMLIKE LITTLE fishes in other people's aquaria, of an infinity of exciting shapes and colors. But I doubt if one could wish for anything more beautiful than young coho salmon. Their natural destiny is to spend one full year in fresh water and their colors, by contrast with the silvery humpback fry and the paler dogs and kings, seem to reflect this. They are not vivid or scintillating or any other adjective that suggests the spectacular; but they have a perfection of matched and subtle detail that is deeply satisfying. All this, combined with the salmonoid's graceful nobility of shape, make them as handsome as any fish that swims.

All salmon and trout fry are handsome little creatures, but the obvious distinguishing marks of the coho are his orange fins, including the tail fin, and the long white outer ray of his anal fin, which readily separates him from the orange-finned cutthroat trout fry. My cohos had olive-brown backs, quite heavily spotted, shading gradually through olive and gold to their silvery bellies. Along their sides were eight or ten heavy black parr marks, narrowly oval in shape and extending well below the lateral line. The whole effect was a velvety richness of smoothly blended color accentuated by the translucent reddish-orange of fins and tail. But my first real surprise in watching them in the tank was that the long white ray of the anal fin was repeated in the dorsal fin; and behind each of these white rays, dramatically emphasizing them, was a black ray. The eyes of my little fish were very large, with golden irises and wide black pupils.

The three fish from Coal Creek quickly sorted themselves into an order of precedence by repeated challenges and chases, then took up fairly regular stations in the tank —No. 1 towards the center, No. 2 behind the big rock in the far right corner, No. 3 near the filter in the opposite corner. They held in mid-water, pectorals moving constantly to control balance and position, dorsal fins erect, bodies and tails gently undulating; young cohos are drift feeders and even the slight flow of water in the tank from the bubbling of the air stone and filter was enough to keep them expectant, readily sampling anything that moved or drifted near them.

Three or four days later I introduced a fourth coho, also from Coal Creek and of the same year's hatch, but about half an inch longer and particularly handsome and strongly colored. He was rather nervous at first and quite easily put to flight by any one of the other three, especially by No. 1, who was a most aggressive little fish. But within a few days he had asserted himself and was firmly holding position in the exact center of the tank—a position he was to hold for over a year, in spite of the attacks of various pretenders and the fairly constant pressure of No. 1.

The little fish showed no hesitation about feeding. May-fly nymphs were their preferred diet and were always taken in mid-water. After a few days they learned to pick up small caddis occasionally from the bottom, though this never seemed to become a regular performance. I had a number of fresh-water snails in the tank which bred very freely; eggs and tiny progeny were spotted all over the glass walls of the tank when I introduced the cohos, and though occasional jellied egg masses persisted, the scattering of young snails promptly disappeared and never again became noticeable.

I had intended at first to maintain a natural diet as nearly as possible, but it was not entirely easy to do so and I soon began to worry about deficiencies in what I was able to provide. To ensure against these I tried supplementary feeding. Scraped beef was acceptable, though most of it got down to the bullheads on the bottom. Of the many commercial fish foods I offered, only dried daphnia stirred any enthusiasm and that was slow because it floats on the surface and the little fish were not much more willing to go up for their food than down. Once they got used to it, though, they came up eagerly, even violently, and it was enough to keep them growing and in good condition.

How much a fisherman can hope to learn from watching small fish in an aquarium, I am not sure, but it is fairly obvious one should be cautious in interpretation. Small May-fly nymphs were unquestionably the favorite food. One can collect these fairly easily in spring and early summer by turning over rocks and driftwood, and most species will quickly lodge on a small aquarium net left in a bucket. It was a simple matter to lift the net out and shake the nymphs free in the aquarium. The little cohos learned almost at once to come to the net and even to grab the nymphs directly from it. Any nymph that swam away was taken immediately in mid-water. But a nymph drifting slowly downwards, without the slightest independent movement, often escaped notice and reached the bottom safely, there to be discovered and eaten by the bullheads. But the descent had to be absolutely motionless. The slightest wriggle drew instant attention and annihilation. I think this is a point well worth the attention of the fly-fisherman, since it suggests again that the eyesight of the salmonoid fishes, even when their attention has been drawn to available feed, is not particularly keen for detailed representation and that independent motion, at least under water, may be essential in attracting attention.

The converse of this was shown even more dramatically by the paddle beetles. From time to time I introduced several small paddle beetles, which swim very actively and come to rest only on the bottom. These were immediately taken and rejected by all the fish in turn; usually they were taken and rejected several times by each fish. Why they were rejected I am not sure; they may bite or may have an unpleasant taste, or both. But in shape they are like nothing else that interested the fish. The only conceivable attraction was in their movement and this seemed to be almost irresistible. Even when a beetle had been swimming around the tank for several hours, repeatedly taken and rejected, one or another of the fish would open his mouth in a bored sort of way, take him in and spit him out again. The beetles never seemed to mind this and cheerfully swam whenever they felt like swimming.

I frequently introduced good numbers of fresh water scuds, which are also quick and active swimmers. They were a little large and a little fast for my fish, who occasionally showed signs of discouragement. I was hopeful that a sufficient number of females would escape to the protection of the rocks and driftwood to have young and maintain a steady food supply, but so far as I know none ever lasted longer than two or three days. In this case there was the attraction of movement and the reward of a satisfying meal and the combination was enough to ensure pursuit to the very end.

The mysid shrimps that I have already described were another introduction that offered movement and a good meal, but their evasive movements were so effective that the little fish actually became discouraged to the point of abandoning pursuit. These little transparent shrimps moved easily and gracefully about the tank and seemed obvious, easy prey. The fish attacked at first with confidence and enthusiasm, but attack after attack failed at the last possible moment as the shrimps flicked themselves sideways, upwards or downwards and then continued serenely on their way. The cohos at first seemed puzzled, but continued to attack. After several minutes of this, the attacks became fewer and more tentative and it was easy to imagine that the fish looked ashamed; certainly their confidence in themselves was seriously disturbed. Finally, the shrimps were swimming calmly about, completely unmolested, while the fish looked sulky and uncomfortable. How long this state of affairs might have persisted, I do not know; eventually the shrimps, which are a brackish-water form, began to feel the effects of the fresh water and their evasive movements became slowed. The fish detected this fairly promptly and resumed pursuit, with greatly increased success; but even so, some shrimps were still alive in the tank after twenty-four hours and many died without being caught.

If one puts all these observations together, the suggestion is that positive individual movement is highly important in attracting attention, that shape and color have only limited importance in comparison with movement and that excessively fast or erratic movement can be discouraging. My own conclusion is that in fishing any sunk fly, slight, repeated movements are highly desirable if they can be imparted to the fly without excessive disturbance. The continuous movement of the rod-top used by the old-fashioned wet-fly man in fishing his fly is almost certainly sound. An occasional twitch of the line by the upstream nymph fisherman may stir fish that would otherwise disregard his offering and the same technique should be even more effective when fishing a drifted wet fly. Even in greased-line fishing some tiny speed-up of the fly at the critical moment may make the difference and stir a fish that would otherwise have let it pass.

Speculations such as these, more idle than otherwise, are only a small part of the pleasure that grows from a natural aquarium. The whole operation encourages ever more detailed search of nearby rivers and creeks and every incidental discovery extends the sense of intimacy that is, I believe, among the richest of a fisherman's satisfactions. Within a year or so one comes across the larvae of all the usual trout-stream insects—May-flies, stone flies, sedges, midges, crane flies and others—and is able to watch their movements and behavior. Such creatures as aquatic beetles, snails and dragonfly nymphs are full of interest. I have no doubt that trout take snails mainly by scraping them off the rocks, but it was interesting to learn that snails can and do crawl along the underside of the surface film. This would make them at least occasionally available to fish at the surface or in mid-water as they drift back towards bottom. Released from an eddy into a strong current, they might well be carried several yards downstream. Much the same applies to the blind and blundering movements of the larger and stronger caddis, which seem to crawl heedlessly over everything in their path and tumble repeatedly into all sorts of awkward predicaments.

The minnow trap that I keep constantly working for me in the river yields many surprises. From January on it produces a daily catch of caddis and May-fly nymphs which gradually falls off as summer advances until by July there are very few indeed. One would expect spring to be the time of high production, but in fact the hatching of many species seems to be at its height in the depths of winter, and spring is the time of their rapid development towards maturity. In the summer months snails and large caddis are still growing down on the bottom, but much of the life is buried in egg patches here and there under the rocks.

The trap is only a tiny, haphazard sampling station, but even so it reveals unexpected movements of fish. If it is placed well the earliest hatches of the various salmon runs will almost certainly yield a sample or two. Sticklebacks show up in seasonal abundance starting in the fall and continuing through until early spring. Sculpins, both spiny and Aleutian, are always there—the trap brings up two or three on most days. But these, too, have their seasonal movements. One night late in April brought a dozen or so, the next night well over a hundred, the third night about twenty and after that the catch was back to normal again.

From time to time I have tried to introduce other fish to the aquarium, but invariably they upset the happy and harmonious relationship that the bullheads and cohos maintained so easily. Sticklebacks were far too pugnacious and soon had the cohos backed miserably into a corner. Young king salmon and dog salmon were readily cowed by the larger cohos and did not feed so readily; one or two established places for themselves, but even when the cohos had accepted them they did not seem to adapt fully to conditions in the tank, possibly because they were on their way down to brackish water when I caught them. I was sorry to have to give up on them because their slender silver shapes, greenish backs, clear fins and heavy parr marks made them a handsome and delicate contrast to the more brightly colored cohos.

The cohos themselves grew steadily and through their first winter were very little behind wild fish in growth— the largest one was somewhat ahead of the average wild fish. There were still four in the tank—the big one who held the center, a slightly smaller but much milder fish, the original No. 1 who remained aggressive in spite of having to yield to his superiors, and a very small one who gladly accepted his lowly standing, took his share of food as he could and otherwise kept out of the way. As spring came I began to worry about them, knowing it was almost time for them to go to sea and expecting the glandular changes of migration to upset them. Early in March both the big fish and No. 1 showed signs of distress—frayed fins, darkened color, a disinclination to feed. This lasted only a few days and recovery seemed complete. On March twenty-sixth I found a steelhead of about three inches in the trap. He was a dark, powerfully built fish, slightly smaller than the big coho, and I thought he might settle in quite readily without causing too much disturbance.

Within a few days it seemed that he had done exactly this. He was a much faster and more active fish than the cohos, ranging freely from top to bottom of the tank, rising to the surface for the dried daphnia with a loud plop and promptly diving down again, balancing and turning on his large pectoral fins, his black-spotted dorsal erect and fan-like, the fins of his underbody white-tipped and vibrant. The big coho chased him in a rather dignified way and effectively kept him from the center of the tank. But the steelhead took these chases calmly, secure in his ability to swim faster and turn faster. Before long he had driven out the second largest coho and taken up his station behind the big rock. It seemed a satisfactory situation all around and I settled down to enjoy his strong markings, his quick, powerful movements and the faint rainbows along his sides.

Then the smallest coho began to turn dark and go off his feed. In his quiet way he was obviously an unhappy fish and on April twenty-second, after one year and eleven days in the tank, he died. At about the same time the second largest coho showed similar symptoms—frayed fins, darkening body, reluctance to feed—and within a month he, too, was dead. Whether these deaths were caused by the frus-

trated need for salt water, by the disturbance of yielding
to the steelhead or by a combination of both factors I am
not sure. I regretted them, but felt that all should be well
with only three fish in the tank.

For two more months all was well. The big coho, plump
and placid, velvety brown and gold, ruled the center of the
tank. The steelhead, growing steadily and brightening from
his original dark colors, ranged everywhere but maintained his station near the big rock and otherwise yielded
to the big fish. Aggressive little No. 1 held his position near
the filter and competed successfully enough with the others
for feed.

The change came overnight. One day the coho was supreme, on the next he was a beaten and dominated fish.
In a way it was not surprising. The steelhead was faster
and more powerful and had grown to the point where
there was little or nothing in size between the two. I supposed it would work out and waited to see the coho accept
a new position. Instead he withdrew, hiding in the weeds
when he could, feeding not at all. His fins became frayed
and he looked thoroughly miserable. The steelhead was
not content with this scale of victory, but continued his
violent attacks whenever he saw the other fish. After three
or four days I saw that the coho's tail was bitten right
back to roots, so I took him out and put him in another
tank, hoping for recovery. It was too late. Fungus attacked
the wounded tail and, though I scraped it away and applied
ointment, he died.

While I still admired the steelhead for his strength and
beauty and quickness, I can't say I liked him after this and
I watched his relationship with little No. 1 very closely.

For two or three weeks all went well. Then the murderer returned to his attacks. I netted him out of the tank, put him in a bucket and took him down to the river, where I released him and followed him with mask and snorkel. He took the change without the slightest discomposure, holding calmly against the current, seeming like any one of the several dozen small pre-migrants that hold behind the wing dam. I followed him for ten or fifteen minutes, then lost him among his fellows.

At the moment the only fish in the tank are two bullheads and No. 1. No. 1 is recovering fast, in color, confidence and fins. I plan to build his ego still further by introducing two or three small cohos of this year's hatch, but I want his tail to grow out first. He is, after all, a remarkable little fish. Once last winter he jumped out through a gap in the canopy of the tank and I picked him up from the carpet, covered with dust and dog hairs and apparently dead. I placed him sadly in the palm of my right hand and there I felt rather than saw a flicker of life in his tiny body. I put him back in the tank and he floated on his back, but his gills moved. I righted him and held him. Within a minute he moved off, within an hour he was feeding and his rate of respiration was almost back to normal. He is still no more than two and a half inches long, but he has a capacity for survival which suggests that he may live out his full three-year life in the tank. I can't claim to be learning much from him and I can't really decide just what is the right thing to do next. I could release him in the river, of course, and set up a whole new batch of fish in the tank. But associations do count for something.

PART SIX

Conclusions

1. *Thoughts while Fishing*

FISHING IS NOT A SPORT I EXPECT EVER TO exhaust or abandon. It has led me and still leads me into too many delights for that. Yet there are times now when I find myself wondering just what it is I am going out to find, with the familiar tackle, in the familiar water at a time made familiar by many past seasons. Is it reasonable to expect some new experience? Or am I just seeking to repeat an old experience? And if so, why? It is disturbing to think such thoughts, even if they fade quickly in the light of experience renewed, experience betrayed or experience unexpectedly new. And it is completely ridiculous to think them because I shall never look upon a river without urgent consideration of the possibilities of finding fish somewhere in it.

It is even more disturbing to think, as I occasionally do, that I may have forgotten more about fish and fishing than I now know—or at all events, more than I now use. Quite recently, for instance, I have caught myself working a fly

close to the surface of a cold mountain lake in early spring
for trivial results and have only later remembered that I
should have been searching the sloughs and beaver dams
and down near the bottom of the shallower bays. Twenty
or thirty years ago I should have done the right thing
almost without thinking and probably come home with a
good catch of fish. Even on rivers I find myself far too
often fishing in some more or less habitual way, pleasant
enough in itself, but not necessarily the best or even the
most satisfying way under the particular circumstances.
Only last month I threw a No. 8 dry fly on a 1x leader
at the heads of several steelhead in succession on a stream
so low it was hardly flowing and was vaguely irritated
when they quietly moved off after the first two or three
casts. A No. 14 spider on 5x would have made a lot more
sense and might even have risen a fish or two, as I well
knew from previous experience. But I didn't think about
it till I got home.

I am left wondering what causes lapses like this? Laziness? Old age? Some lack of concern about catching fish?
No doubt all these three play a part. But over and above
them all is a measure of obstinacy mixed with some faint
conceit that one should be able to *force* the fish, against
all the probabilities, to accept one's own terms. The more
sensible alternatives are, for the moment, less attractive
precisely because they have succeeded in the past and probably would do so again.

Often, too, I am ungrateful enough to be irritated by the
illogical behavior of the fish I do catch. One October day
last year I was fishing the tail of a pool full of spawning
salmon when a good trout came short to a lazily drifted fly

that I hoped looked something like a caddis grub. I tried again and he would not come back. The obvious conclusion was that he was interested in nothing but salmon eggs, so I put up a small orange fly, drifted it down and hooked him immediately and securely. In his stomach were a dozen snails and two large caddis grubs; not a single salmon egg. I felt then that the whole business was completely over my head and always would be; I wondered how I had the nerve to form any theories at all, let alone proclaim them.

With a little rationalization and the natural return of confidence, one gets over these setbacks—as a matter of fact, I have had to get over this particular one several times before, though never quite so dramatically presented. I have even developed a theory that trout don't care very much for salmon eggs if plenty of other good food is available. But if so, why reject a fly that looks like a caddis and take one that looks like a salmon egg? No doubt because natural salmon eggs weren't as plentiful as they seemed to be and this particular artificial one came along at just the right moment to meet with favor. Almost anything can be explained, if one tries hard enough, but fortunately a fisherman's explanations aren't usually open to proof, so they don't register very strongly even on his own mind and he finds himself free to go out the next time in the same happy state of confusion and doubt.

I often wonder why, when we are so anxious to give our quarry credit for cunning, intelligence, even wisdom, we are so reluctant to admit that he may have individuality. There is, after all, no reason why a fish shouldn't prefer a nice light salmon egg after heavy, hard-shelled feeding on snails and caddis, or even vice versa. And we don't really

know what is going on down there. He may have been
chased off the redds by several angry salmon in succession
without his heart's desire, only to have it come drifting
conveniently by him in the form of bright wool and
feathers. If we told ourselves more fairy stories like this,
we might fish with much more verve and originality.

Sometimes, and always with the greatest respect, I blame
old Frederick Halford for much of our dullness. No one
has ever taken greater pains with exact imitation, not
merely of a species of fly but with precision as to its sex
and state of development. He has harsh words to say about
those "awful monstrosities called fancy flies" even while
admitting that they occasionally take fish; and I suspect he
would have been heartily ashamed of killing a fish on a
light olive in the midst of a hatch of dark olives. Generations of fishermen have followed him or at least paid lip
service to his theories. Yet Halford didn't really recom-
mend this. He was careful to point out that most of his
fishing was done on waters where "the education of the
fish has reached a very high standard and where, day by
day, from the opening to the closing of the season, flies dry
and wet, floating and sunk, are cast with more or less precision over every fish." What would he have thought of
our wild western fish and their lack of opportunity for
sophistication? "I have not had many opportunities of trying the more favoured localities where the visit of the fly-
fisherman is of rare occurrence and the flashing of the
glittering gut an unusual circumstance; but where I have
done so, the conclusion arrived at has been that the selec-
tion of the fly is of far less importance and the accuracy
and delicacy of far greater importance." Wild fish, he says,

in effect, will be far less tolerant of any sight of the angler or his moving rod, but far more tolerant of a heavy leader or a poor representation of the natural fly. I am not sure that experience fully supports these ideas, but at least here is a suggestion from the highest possible authority that exact imitation isn't the whole story, even on streams that have abundant hatches of aquatic insects.

I am afraid most of us who are ordinary run-of-the-mill fishermen, fishing rather varied waters under varying conditions, have to count on having our most cherished theories upset from time to time, and I doubt if we should complain about it or resent it. Undoubtedly fish have patterns of behavior that are roughly predictable and we can afford to take pride in our understanding of these patterns and the successes that grow from it. But fortunately we are working always with an infinity of variables that would drive any scientist to distraction—season, temperature, current, light, the aberrations of the fish themselves, their senses and perceptions and perhaps even the aberrations of insects. We may be able to tidy all this into a nice workable theory from time to time and gain greatly from it, but I do not think we need feel ashamed or rejected when such a theory falls apart. It is better to summon back a youthful contempt for experience and some of youth's keenness and boldness in experiment.

There are careful and scientific anglers who have developed theories, tested them and in large measure proved them; no one owes more to these fine sportsmen than I do. From time to time I develop some small theory of my own about how and why and where fish should take, and it seems to hold up fairly well over the years. It would be absurd to suggest that I don't enjoy these minor triumphs. I enjoy the ones that fail, too, even in the moment of failure. I still get ideas of this sort and become impatient to try them out under the right conditions, but I no longer expect quite so much of them; if there is a measure of success I know it will not change very much—at best, I shall have a slightly different fly pattern or technique of presenting it that will work well under the right conditions, if I happen to recognize the conditions and remember the pattern or the technique.

If fishing were simply a matter of catching fish or forming and testing angling theories, I think I should have given it up long ago. Nor is it simply a matter of exciting and beautiful surroundings, the splendor and loveliness of running water and the attraction that rivers have for creatures of all kinds, including man. These are a large and important part of it all, but one can enjoy them without going fishing and I often do. I think perhaps the lasting charm of fishing is in the pace of the sport and in the fish themselves.

The pace of fly-fishing, unlike that of most sports, can be quite easily controlled to suit one's mood. One can work hard at it if one chooses—wading upstream with a dry fly, plowing through brush from pool to pool, climbing around steep banks and rock bluffs to get at good water can add up to the hardest possible kind of day, if that seems desirable. But one can always get a fair measure of fishing without going to such extremes. Fishing can be dangerous, if one chooses to make it so, by wading heavy current over a bad bottom or taking chances in a small boat. These things have their place in the sport, but one can always cut them down to size and keep them under control. Most days of wading on most western streams produce a moment or two of breathlessness, psychological as well as physical, but the momentary concern is more likely to be over the risk of a wet backside than any risk of drowning.

The fish are fast, of course, some five times as fast as a man in their reactions, but fortunately they don't always use this advantage. When they do one may suffer disaster or recover with a sense of triumph; in either event there should be a memory that will last. For the rest, there is nearly always time to do things smoothly, with whatever grace and style one can attain by practice, and this seems important.

In the last analysis, though, it must be the fish themselves that make fishing—the strangeness and beauty of fish, their often visible remoteness, their ease in another world, the mystery of their movements and habits and whims. The steelhead lying in the summer pool, the brown trout rising under the cut bank, the Atlantic salmon rolling over his lie, the bass breaking in the lily pads, the grayling glimpsed in the rapid, the enormous unseen trout cruising the lake's drop-off, all these are irresistible temptations to anyone who has held a rod. It is not that one wants to kill, though kill one may. The appeal is more nearly that of hidden treasure, except that this treasure has life and movement and uncertainty beyond anything inanimate. The thought in the mind is: "Let me try for him." The desire is to stir the reaction, respond to it, control it; to see the mystery close by in the water, perhaps to handle it, to admire, to understand a little. Perhaps it adds up to nothing more than a primitive curiosity, but if so it remains powerful and lasting.

I wonder how many times I have explored the nature
and meaning of fishing in somewhat this way and what
different conclusions I have reached from time to time?
The differences do not matter very much—they merely
reflect differences of mood and experience. But the need
to examine and explore does seem important. Angling was
once the quiet sport of a few men. At various times it has
been considered immoral, self-indulgent, degenerate, at
others a harmless aberration, justifying mildly humorous
persecution. These must have been times, too, when no one
paid very much attention and the quiet men were left to go
their quiet ways in peace; these were probably the best
times of all. But now the sport seems to have taken the
public fancy as few sports ever have; practically every
family in North America has its enthusiastic fisherman and
one in every two or three of us has at least a casual interest
in the sport. It has become necessary to wonder how good
fishing can be found for so many and from this comes the
even sharper need to wonder what fishing is all about.

Obviously fishing is different things to different people
and that is just as well. But the sources of its persistent
fascination probably do not vary much. Highest among
them I would place the impossibility, for nearly all of us
anyway, of achieving anything approaching complete and
regular success, in spite of the delightful delusion that success of this sort is never far away.

The barriers between fish and fisherman are many and
significant. We share the same world, but limit ourselves to
different parts of it. We breathe, move, feed, sleep and, no
doubt, think quite differently in entirely different elements.
The fisherman's brain and his power of reasoning give him

an important advantage in all of this, but it is limited by the most important barrier of all—the surface film of river or lake or sea. Only rarely are we able to see even approximately what a fish does in his natural environment under natural conditions; still more rarely, even under the most favorable circumstances, can we hope to see *exactly* what he does and reach a valid conclusion as to exactly how and why he has done it. The rest is inference and deduction, often on very slim grounds indeed. Most of us subscribe happily to the idea that we are just naturally good at this sort of thing—better than a fish anyway—so the illusion of impending success is happily sustained. We cheerfully accept the terms and go forth again and again, expecting to solve the unseen and unkown by some new and ingenious change in our own attitude towards the matter. The fish doesn't change very much. He doesn't need to.

There are plenty of reasons in all this for me to go on fishing. I may have exhausted a few forms of fishing and satisfied myself that I have the right ideas about a few others. But there are always intriguing possibilities unexplored or incompletely explored.

I am, for instance, not nearly satisfied yet as to the real attitude of winter steelhead towards a floating fly, simply because I haven't so far had the fortitude and determination to give it a thorough try. The logic of water temperatures and the apparent mood of the fish themselves are all against it, but then one could make a fairly logical case against summer steelhead taking a floating fly as well as they do. For reasons best known to themselves winter steelhead frequently come up and strike at the bobbers of bait and spinner fishermen; and the logic of that is that they should come at least as readily to a floating fly of the right size and pattern—not necessarily round, plastic and red and white.

Just as intriguing, though I am less likely to give it a fair trial, is the possibility of doping a fly with some attractive scent, especially for winter steelhead. Whether the ethics of this bear examination, I am not quite sure, but the question is a good one and someone should answer it satisfactorily. Various magic scents do appear on the market from time to time, with claims of powers of attraction only a little less dramatic than those of the better-known brands of lady's perfumes. I once bought one and seem to recall that I did anoint a few flies with it. Unfortunately the bottle fell on its side in a file of unanswered letters and the magic potion leaked out past the cork. The results of this effort must, therefore, be considered inconclusive.

Among trappers and fishermen this sort of preparation has since antiquity been planned to serve two purposes in deception—the destruction or concealment of human scent and the substitution of some positive attraction. Kwakiutl Indians of the west coast, for instance, used to boil their wooden halibut hooks with spruce roots and devil's-club bark to reduce human scent; modern trappers boil their traps in similar brews and nearly always use some potent mixture of animal scents near their sets. In spite of sound scientific evidence that migrating fish are repelled by minute traces of human and other predators' scents, I have experienced nothing to suggest that feeding or resting fish are disturbed by human scents. Every fisherman has caught fish time and again immediately after changing a fly or lure. I have held my hand in the water directly above spawning and resting salmon and observed little or no reaction from the fish. When I am under water steelhead and other fry frequently swim up right between my bare hands, and trout of all sizes, as well as salmon and steelhead, seem to close in behind my flippers. But an attractive or stimulating scent might well be a different matter, especially for reluctant fish like winter steelhead. It probably plays its part in the success of salmon roe and other baits. My preference would be for something fairly simple and natural, such as eulachon oil or even sardine oil. But it sounds like a messy business and I may leave it to some more conscientious fisherman.

These are some of the thoughts that go through my mind when I am fishing. On a blank day? Well, no. It was a late November day and I was looking around in the hope that I might find an early-running winter steelhead. A big goshawk was screaming at me from one of the spruces on the Lower Island. He kept at it intermittently from the time he first saw me until I had fished almost down to him, and I thought his screams a lovely, wild, defiant sound. As I came close he turned clumsily on his branch, like a tame parrot, screamed once more and flew across the river to another tall tree. A few, very few, spawning salmon were still alive. Dippers worked among the rocks, a kingfisher chattered along the far side of the river, goldeneyes, mergansers, mallards and a few gulls were finding the remnants of the salmon runs. The Main Island Pool was full of cutthroats, clean bright and full of fight, though my gear was much too heavy. I kept three of them because it was a Friday and resolved to come back in a day or two with more appropriate gear.

I wondered then if there may not be times when the rod, like the gun, is an encumbrance, a responsibility that interferes with the simpler and keener pleasures of seeing and hearing and feeling and finding. One can travel farther and faster without it and the eyes and mind are free to turn attention to the whole scene instead of concentrating on some small fraction of it.

I decided the comparison would not quite stand, if only because the water hides so much. The fly rod tests the unseen. Without it I should have still suspected early-winter steelhead lurking in the pools; without it I should never have suspected that the Main Island Pool was full of bright immature cutthroats, averaging about fifteen inches long and feeding almost entirely on snails. I should not care to miss such discoveries.

2. *Thoughts under Water*

Modern inventions in fly-fishing tackle do not impress me greatly. Glass rods have power and lightness and cheapness, as well as a measure of durability, but there is really nothing they will do that cane rods cannot do just as well. Synthetic lines have their virtues, but silk lines in competent hands will do just about everything that can be claimed for synthetic lines and they left us free from the awful modern complication of weights, and comparatively free from the wretched decision of which lines to take along for any given set of conditions. Synthetic leaders are stronger for their thickness, but in most respects they are inferior to silkworm gut and it is a pity that their cheapness, convenience and availability persuade us to use them. Good fly reels have needed no improvement in my fishing lifetime. And nothing much has been added to the art of fly-tying, dry or wet, since hair wings first became popular.

But the invention of the wet suit, mask, snorkel and flippers is in an entirely different category. It has added an entirely new dimension to my life and I am eternally grateful to the men who developed the gear and techniques to their present state of perfection. For the first time a fisherman can go through the surface film in comfort and stay there just as long as he likes. For the first time a man can experience some of the sensations of a fish and can know the bottom of a river as well as he knows its surface. Just a few years ago nothing of the sort was possible, even for the hard-hat diver who walked the bottom at the end of his air line. Today anyone can do it.

Even when I decided to invest in the necessary equipment I had only the slightest idea of what to expect from it. I supposed I should find cold water somewhat less cold, that I should be able to poke about briefly here and there in the quieter parts of the streams and see fish better than I had seen them before. Instead I found myself immediately transported from the world of air to the world of water and at least as comfortable in the new world as the old. True, there were occasional gaggings and sputterings as I learned the rhythms of breathing through a snorkel, moments of doubt as I experimented to find just how much weight I must carry on my belt to give me approximately neutral buoyancy, some aching of the knees and leg muscles as I accustomed myself to the use of flippers. But these were trivial discomforts that serve only to emphasize the miraculous thing that was happening to me.

Many years ago, when the children were small and learning to swim, I built a wing dam out into the river by piling up rocks and boulders. It was a laborious process, as we had no other machinery than a horse and a set of blocks, but the result has stood firmly against the freshets of more than twenty years and now the controlled river runs much of the time at a height that just breaks over the dam in three or four bubbling runs, while the main force of the current swings past the point in a formidable sweep of power.

This was a natural place to learn familiarity with the simple mechanics of swimming and diving, but to my delight it was also a place full of life and beauty. The moment one's masked face is under the surface film, the everyday world is lost. The body in its buoyant suit stretches out in the enclosing water; flippers, given depth by the weight belt, have a slow, easy power that is much like walking. The water, enclosing, is all-supporting. The body has no weight, only an easy fluidity of motion. One moves lazily, because the gain of violent movement is slight and exhausting. It is easy to rest, more completely than in the softest of beds, by relaxing every muscle and accepting the water's infinitely gentle support.

As I move up from the tail of the pool below the dam there are always under-yearling cohos and steelheads about me, lively little fish that care nothing at all for my strange shape and stranger movements. They will swim within inches of my outstretched hands and sometimes between them. Occasionally one seems to swim deliberately and curiously towards the face mask, perhaps attracted by the movement of the wondering eyes behind it.

A little farther up the pool, along the edge of the current that comes past the point of the dam, the fish are yearling steelheads, four, five and six inches long. During the early part of the season, in the more sheltered water, there is a scattering of greenbacked king salmon fingerlings, most of them within weeks of going to sea. I pass among them gently, looking down at the bullheads and caddis larvae on the sandy bottom. To my right the current races unevenly over a bottom of round boulders that disappears in blue-green distance. If I glance up I can see the rippled, bouncing surface.

At the head of the pool, in the plunging bubbles of the runs and among the big boulders of the dam, there are larger fish, seven- and eight-inch rainbows, probably premigrant steelheads in their second or even third year, and two or three sizable trout between twelve and fifteen inches. This is where I hold, schooled with the fish, my hands moving occasionally like pectoral fins, flippers moving when they must to keep me in station. The smaller fish seem to accept me completely. The larger ones hold station or continue their affairs, but they are aware of me and will move away if I reach a hand within eighteen inches or a foot of them.

For several weeks this summer there were two large fish that held station close under the dam, both rainbows, each about fourteen inches long. The larger was a firm, bright, deep fish, the other a slender fish with a marked red stripe along its side. They seemed entirely different types and I suspected that the slender one was a resident river rainbow while the other may have been an estuary fish that had moved up. When the river was high they often moved back and forth between the runs that broke over the dam and sometimes held station facing downstream among the larger boulders, searching the drift that came back in the underwater eddies. Even in this position they would allow me to approach very closely provided I did not seem to block off the obvious way of escape from among the rocks. The moment I showed any sign of doing so they darted past me into the open water of the pool.

Needless to say I became fond of these fish and I like to think that they got used to me, or at least became satisfied that I was harmless. As a fly-fisherman I was impressed first of all by their readiness to move about in response to comparatively slight changes in river height and even, it seemed, to range back and forth between preferred stations in search of the best one. But they did hold, and hold very firmly at times, especially in the violent turbulence just off the point of the dam. The boulders here are very large, some of them as much as three or four feet in diameter, and the current has dug a deep rock-floored race just beyond them. Bubbles break down in intermittent showers from the build-up behind the shoulder of the dam and nothing is constant except movement; but one can find a handhold on one or other of the big boulders readily enough and cling there, tossed and tumbled like the fish themselves.

For they are tossed and tumbled, lifted and dropped, by the swirls and eddies and surges. I had imagined trout holding in such a place well down on the bottom, taking shelter among the round rocks and darting out to intercept drifting feed. These fish did not. They held just above the tops of the boulders and accepted the current with their whole bodies. They held station with the power of their bodies, even as I held with my hand's grip, and they were twisted and turned and battered by it, even as I was.

But they were able to move in it as I was not—up or down
or sideways with little effort, intercepting and swallowing
things too fast and small for me to see. How long a fish
may hold in such an active station I do not know, but I
have watched them for fifteen or twenty minutes at a
stretch and when some clumsy motion of mine displaced
them, they returned almost immediately.

While these fish can move with a flick of their tails from
the strong current into the easier flow behind the dam, I
doubt if it would normally occur to me to search such
heavy water with a fly. From now on, of course, I shall
do so. A deeply drifted fly would be the most likely to
bring a faithful response, but drifting it accurately would
not be easy. A wet fly hung from above would be the
next choice, but I doubt if the chances of hooking the
fish securely would be better than fifty per cent. A good
big dry-fly cast upstream would almost certainly produce
a rise, but again the chances of hooking the fish would not
be good, since he would be responding through some four
feet of very fast water.

Underwater thoughts such as these are purely academic
and altogether kindly towards the fish. I have promised
myself to kill nothing under water and to disturb whatever
lives there as little as possible. It wouldn't seem right to
watch the fish behind the dam through an afternoon and
go out and catch them in the evening. But academic knowledge has its uses and I have no reservations about applying
what generalizations I learn under water when I am back
above the surface film again and fishing in the ordinary
way.

When I ask myself why I have taken to the mask and

snorkel with such enthusiasm after all these years, the first answer that comes to my mind is: curiosity. To that I must add: love of the fish and love of the water. But I had no idea it would be so beautiful. I had no idea I would see so much or so clearly. I had no idea it would be possible to move about a great rushing river so freely and easily or that the human body could adapt so completely and readily to flowing water. We have disadvantages, of course. Through the best of masks our forward-seeing eyes give only restricted vision. We cannot begin to make headway against anything more than the most moderate current. It is rarely possible to approach a fish unseen, so one is always left wondering whether its behavior is entirely natural. But in spite of all this one can see so much and so much more thoroughly than is ever possible from above the surface that it is fair to say one becomes an authentic part of the underwater world.

The underwater world is friendly and confiding, which is why I do not want to bring death or unnecessary disturbance into it. Fry and fingerlings and yearlings seem to have no fear at all of the hovering figure in the black suit. Larger trout are wary, especially when they are freshly up from salt water, but they accept the intrusion so long as the approach is not too close and in time they seem to understand there is no danger. The salmon are very nervous when they first come in, decreasingly so as they approach maturity. Rivers, even big ones, are narrow and shallow places compared to the ocean depths and a diver in a wet suit must look like nothing but danger.

Sometimes I wonder if a suit of some other color than black might disturb the fish less; the effect of black under water is a shadowy gray, a good deal like that of a seal or a predatory fish. But it seems to me that the attention of the fish is always for the face mask and the eyes behind it—especially, I imagine, for the eyes. They watch me, eye to eye, and scatter from my slowest approach, but if I turn and look back I see them as often as not regrouped close under my moving flippers; often, too, a fish will hold almost indefinitely while one is watching him from a safe distance, then disappear immediately the eyes are turned away.

"What are you doing down there?" small boys ask me along the river. "Getting lures off the bottom?"

"No," I answer. "Looking for fish."

"Find any?"

"Sure, lots."

"What do you do when you find them?"

"Just watch them."

This final answer rarely satisfies and I could, I suppose, give others equally truthful—that I am checking on the runs, looking over the river bottom, testing the set of the currents, trying to solve a lifetime of mysteries. Some of my friends urge me to get an underwater camera and no doubt it would be nice at times to have one. But I would rather be without encumbrances and complications beyond the essential ones, at least while everything is so fresh and new. I want to be free to watch and think and feel and perhaps to come a little closer to understanding what the underwater world is really like.

3. *The Freedom of the River*

THE FIRST FINE FREEDOM OF THE RIVER is not entirely without its anxieties. One is aware of the power of the equipment, which largely removes the swimmer's familiar warnings of cold and fatigue. The ease of breathing with mask and snorkel is such that any sudden interruption is more disconcerting than swimming without such aids, at least until such time as the proper reactions have become automatic and unfailing. I found myself looking with doubt and even apprehension at rapids I have often swum safely in nothing more than a pair of trunks.

In time and as experience builds, a sense of proportion returns. But it is still important to remain respectful of the equipment and its power, to say nothing of the river itself. One can judge the power of a current or the run of a pool and its eddies with substantial accuracy from above the surface film and it is as well to do so quite thoroughly and deliberately before committing oneself further. It is important also to consider the water carefully *each* time, even when it is familiar water, because a comparatively small rise in the river can produce a marked increase in the speed of its currents and may knock out many sheltered holding places.

But when all this is said, and acted upon, the freedom of the river is very real. One can move about it in comfort and safety and use all its tricks and vagaries to astonishing advantage.

A suited diver, even with his full weight belt, draws no more than a foot or so of water. Yet even in a foot of water he often need only turn his head slightly to be looking straight into the flowing depths where the fish lie. Even in three or four feet of water he can reach down to rocks or limbs on the bottom and hold or propel himself against quite powerful currents. In still deeper water he can dive down to some favorable boulder, grip it and hold briefly while he looks about him. With tanks, of course, he can do much more than this, but in swift streams tanks are an encumbrance that inhibits rather than increases freedom.

Once under the surface film it makes little difference whether one is over two feet or twenty feet of water—the feeling of being down there, in that other world, is complete. Along the edges of the rapids and pools the great boulders stand out boldly from among the rocks of the bottom, with white bubbles dancing round them while the drift flows endlessly by in the streamy water. Beyond the last boulder, perhaps thirty feet upstream, and away to the side there is blue-green infinity, waiting to be pushed back and become finite as one moves slowly upstream or swiftly downstream.

I prefer to work upstream whenever I can because one approaches the fish from behind and there is more time to see and better chance to see without being seen. One picks a way over the rocky bottom, now moving up behind the shelter of a massive boulder, now slipping between two boulders so close together there seems no room to pass, now sliding over a run of current to find more shelter or to glance out into the deeper water. Sunlight streaks into the water through the trees of the riverbank, and yearling steelheads and cohos glitter like silver leaves as they turn and twist in the flow. One passes among them and comes suddenly out of the greenness into a lighter world where an eddy has built a white sand bottom. There are bullheads, large and small, perched in the hollows of the sand, the large ones (all of six or eight inches long) looking very formidable with their wide jaws, fanlike orange pectorals and sharply tapered bodies, the small ones speckled and perky. Trails of crawling caddis mark the sand and fresh-water mussels thrust up from it. At the upstream end, where current meets countercurrent, more little cohos and steelheads flicker as they intercept the drift of tiny life that is carried to them by the stream.

Above the eddy are more boulders, deeper water and stronger current. But there is intermittent shelter and it is easy enough to work out to the largest boulder, find a hand grip and push out into the edge of the main flow. Surges of current tear at mask and shoulders and a con-stant race of bubbles hides everything at first. Close against the boulder, just under the source of the bubbles, is a glassy flow of undisturbed water and through it one is suddenly looking at a fine trout. He is close enough for every spot to be counted. The current swirls him and the swimmer's body is tossed by an echoing surge. The trout moves up easily and his white mouth opens to intercept something unseen. He settles back towards bottom, swirls up again, settles back again and yawns.

It is a quiet sort of pastime, much like wandering through some strange, beautiful and unending garden where the fish seem exotic creatures miraculously and perfectly naturalized, ideally matched to place and setting. Nothing is altogether unexpected—everything is as it must and should be, yet everything is also new and breath-taking experience, a wonder of seeing that never stales. It would be wrong to say that one loses all sense of time; I am usually quite concerned about time when I am swimming and diving. But an hour seems like twenty minutes and if I think I have been gone an hour I have been gone three hours.

It is not easy to see all of the river. Most of the pools call for quite careful planning and a good deal of swimming; one learns gradually, by trial and error and ingenious calculation. Often it is impossible to come on the fish in any way but by drifting swiftly downstream, which is the worst way, but every boulder that reaches up to the surface, every little indentation along the shore line is shelter and protection. One can slide in there, hold and peer out into the flowing deeps. On weekends, when part of the massive turbine flow is shut off, the sheltered places are more numerous and one can make way upstream almost anywhere along the shore line. Often, too, discoveries made in low water serve almost equally well at the river's full flow.

The canyon of the Campbell has always been a place of some mystery. From its outlet by the powerhouse to the sharp corner where Elk Falls drop ninety feet into a rock-sided bowl is just a mile. Through most of that distance the canyon walls are forbiddingly steep, often sheer, and carry to a height at least as great as that of the falls. Over the years I have several times worked my way down into the canyon, but have always found it impossible to travel very far—upstream or down, the way is soon barred by the drop of a rock cliff into six or eight feet of water. Yet the whole length of the canyon is open to the movement of fish and it has always seemed that there would be strange and wonderful things to be seen there.

Stan Douglas, my patient and sympathetic instructor in the arts of the wet suit and mask, suggested that a trip through the canyon to the foot of the falls might be a pleasant outing one sunny Sunday in July. I agreed most warmly and four of us started off together soon after ten in the morning—Barry Ross, Carol Ross, Stan and I. We carried our weight belts, which was foolish, but no diver likes to be without one; Stan and I had no protection for our feet beyond the boots of our wet suits, which was doubly foolish. But sometimes one has to learn the hard way.

The great gates at the dam were shut and there was very little water flowing through the canyon when we started— no more than a twelve-inch pipe would hold—but we knew there would be a release of water at around 2 P.M. for the benefit of the tourists at the falls. We cut behind the powerhouse, put on our gear and slid into the quiet water of the first great pool. The pool is an ideal start. It twists between sheer rock walls for over two hundred yards. It is enormously deep. In many places we could not see bottom on that day, even though we dove down the shafts of sunlight in search of it. At one point a rock barrier rising to within a few feet of the surface almost cuts it in two, though there are deep and narrow passages on either side. A little beyond, the rock walls crowd very close together then spread apart again. We could see the bottom now, thirty or forty feet down, and the pool gradually shallowed from here to the pile of tumbled rock that made its head. Little falls came glittering down through the rocks, gathering to a respectable flow at one corner where a number of steelhead and coho fingerlings were schooled. Right under the fall itself were two red-sided rainbows of about twelve inches. Through the body of the pool we had seen only a few scattered steelhead yearlings, though there was a school of a thousand or more mixed fingerlings by the rock where we started and a small school of mature humpbacks across from them.

For the next quarter of a mile the canyon floor was a formidable mass of broken rock over which we clambered uncomfortably in the hot sun. The short pools were not worth swimming, though we cooled off in one or two of them, and the narrow channels and cataracts of water among the rocks were too swift and small to swim. Then the pools became larger and we intermittently swam and climbed. The canyon walls were sometimes very close, craggy and sheer, and at other times sloped almost gently back through forest from the bare rock at the water's edge. The bottoms of the pools were covered with round, water-worn rocks, but great rugged boulders around which we happily turned and twisted rose up amongst them. At one point the canyon walls came within forty or fifty feet of each other and I expected great depth, but there was only a bare rock floor, quite shallow and seamed with quartz.

The high July sun streamed into every pool and near the head of each, where the current flow rippled the surface, it spread a mesh of light like gill-net web over the boulders and bottom, shimmering and beautiful. As we moved up, the red-sided rainbows seemed to become more numerous and there were still steelhead—or perhaps resident rainbow—fingerlings, though I could see no cohos among them.

We came at last to the long pool on the bend, three-quarters of a mile from the start and a quarter of a mile from the falls. I had been there before and recognized it easily, not without relief. The red-sided rainbows here were both larger and fewer than I remembered and there was one clean, bright, deep fish of about sixteen inches that had almost certainly run up from tidal water.

Above the long pool are two more big pools and then the falls pool itself. Each pool is separated from the one below it by a great pile of massive rocks and boulders, each pile higher and steeper than the one before it and the boulders in each more stupendously huge. The canyon walls were very high and steep, sheer rock precipices, higher than the falls themselves, and all over the bottom of the pools was a scattering of freshly broken rock, uncomfortable warning that even on this bright and sunny day the canyon might not be without its hazards. But we came safely to the falls pool at last, sat briefly to admire the narrow stream of the falls, waved to the tourists, tiny and distant on the lookout, and slid into the pool.

Elk Falls at full flood is a tremendous sight. Spray drives

up hundreds of feet into the air. The water crashes over in a thunder of white, filling the narrow bowl between the rock walls and hiding all sight of the pool itself. Even at normal summer level the fall is formidable and spectacular. I had supposed that these plunging millions of tons of water over hundreds of years must have worn a pool far deeper than any we had seen so far. But the pool was comparatively shallow, not over twenty feet in the main part, with a bottom of round boulders that must churn like marbles in a bowl at high water. Right under the fall is a massive rock outcrop and close beside it a huge boulder that has been scooped by the rush of water into the smooth and elegant form of a chair molded for a giant. Beyond the falls, in the dark and narrow cleft that runs in by the lookout, the water is considerably deeper, though even here we could see the bottom.

A school of the biggest red-sided trout we had seen was cruising the pool. There were twenty or thirty altogether, from twelve to sixteen or eighteen inches long, the larger ones thin, soft-looking and rather dark. It was impossible to imagine that they were anything but resident fish, living out their lives in that dark and turbulent spot, perhaps dropping back to the pools below when the water was higher. This conclusion in turn confirmed the thought that the red-sided fish of the other pools and of the main river below the canyon must also be resident stock.

We knew we had been a long while on the way up, so we left the Falls Pool after fifteen or twenty minutes and started down. Going down was easier, as we could twist and hump our way through some of the narrow channels between the pools instead of walking. Just below the long pool the afternoon flow of water caught up to us. Barry had just gone down a chute about six feet long. Stan, starting down, caught a ride that plowed him under, ripped his suit and helmet, tore off both flippers and took his knife. He found his feet, caught one flipper as it swept past and signaled to Carol and me to find another way, which we did.

From there on the added water was a help, though we treated it with respect, clambering round the rocks at two or three points to avoid the rougher falls. The sudden flow of water seemed to have brought out far more fish in every pool than we had seen on the way up. There is not much doubt that the diversion of water around the canyon to the powerhouse has lost the Campbell much of its most valuable rearing water for migratory fish.

We reached the rock behind the powerhouse about five hours after we had started from it, a little battered, a little weary and with tender feet. Carol said she couldn't wait to get out of her monkey suit. I wanted a smoke. Stan said I had the queerest ideas about what would make a nice quiet Sunday swim, and it was only later I remembered that the idea was his, not mine. But I felt that a blank in my life had been filled. For the first time I had been over the whole length of the Campbell, from the sea to the foot of the falls. I suppose someone might reasonably ask: "Is that important?" I could find some fine, high-sounding reasons for its importance, but I am not much interested in them. What is truly important is that the river has no more blank and doubtful spaces in my mind's consideration of it.

4. *Return of the Salmon*

Working from above the surface film a fisherman learns, in time, a great deal about where and how fish lie in a stream. Such learning is in many ways the greatest test of his ability as a fisherman. On a familiar stream he will work certain favorite spots whenever he can. On a strange stream his eye will search the surface of the water, the conformation of pools and runs, and experience will recognize signs that under similar conditions elsewhere have meant fish or no fish, large fish or small fish. Every so often experience will be proved unsound, but even in this new experience will be born and so, by degrees, the total of experience becomes very large.

I count my own experience along these lines quite fair, but one short summer and fall of working under the surface film has shown me that it is remarkably incomplete and that my understanding has often been faulty. The list of surprises that my own river, the Campbell, has given me is so long, so humiliating and so full of pleasures that I scarcely know where to start it. Perhaps it is logical to start with the little fish, pre-migrant fingerlings and yearlings, fish which are often a nuisance to the fly-fisherman but which are, after all, the future of his sport.

I use the term "fingerlings" to mean young fish that are spending their first year of life in the river—in the Campbell they may be young steelheads, cohos, cutthroats or king salmon and will usually be under three inches in length. By "yearlings" I mean fish that are spending a second year in the river before going to sea—usually fish of four to eight inches that are almost certain to be young steelheads, though a few may be young cutthroats.

Fishing experience and observation from above the surface had persuaded me that fingerlings were usually to be found spread out over shallow water of moderate flow, while the stronger yearlings would be feeding busily in deeper and faster water, often near the heads of pools and runs. My first excursions under water confirmed this fairly well. Steelhead yearlings were abundantly in evidence, not merely at the heads of the pools and runs, but in the swifter water along the sides of the pools and along the edges of rapids and even to some extent in the deep water in the body of the pools. They are, in fact, just about everywhere there is a chance of finding food drifting down with the current.

The little fingerling steelheads were also scattered widely through many parts of the stream, though they showed a clear preference for slower and shallower water than their older relatives. With them and among them nearly always

were a few coho fingerlings and, early in the season, a
few handsome greenbacked king salmon fingerlings. These
last had pretty well disappeared by early August, which
was to be expected as most of them spend no more than
a few months in fresh water. But all young cohos spend
a full year in fresh water, and I was a little surprised that
they were not more numerous.

The explanation came by degrees. The first surprise was
the very large school of fingerlings at the start of the first
long pool in the canyon. It turned out that this school was
always there in exactly the same station, just beside the
rock around the corner from the powerhouse and the surge
pool. It totaled between one and two thousand fish, of
which at least ninety-five per cent were cohos. The flow
of water off the rock is barely perceptible, made of whatever little current comes out of the canyon at the normal
summer shut-off and some back eddy from the flow over
the lip of the surge pool. The school holds over water two
or three feet deep, but this is only a shelf and the protection of almost unlimited depth is close at hand.

Stan Douglas made the next discovery under the first
bent of the bridge at the head of the Sandy Pool. He
swam to a large brush pile that hangs there and immediately
signaled me to join him. Peering through the underwater
tangle of the brush pile we could see the dim shapes of
a few small fish, then more and more and more of them.
Nearly all were cohos, though a few sticklebacks of about
the same size held amongst them. This again proved to
be a station that is held most faithfully. The little fish
never leave it unless the river's flow is shut down so far
that the brush pile is almost high and dry, when they

move out into open water nearby. Again it is a station of very moderate flow, with excellent protection.

Just a few days ago I swam and dived through the large pool that has been dug out of the north bank of the Campbell for the pulp-mill water intake. The upstream third of this pool, some two hundred feet long by fifty or sixty feet wide, has been in existence for several years and its bottom is thickly grown with weed. A moderate current flows back from the river under the protecting log boom at the mouth of the pool. The rest of the pool is less than a year old, and large sheets of canvas, hung from the log boom, hold any significant flow of current away from it.

I swam the length of the boom first, looking for large fish, and found them; several very large cutthroats were lying just inside the boom, where the current turned against some huge overturned concrete anchors from the downstream wall of the old channel; a few ripening humpback salmon were holding in the swiftly flowing river pool outside the boom. The new section of the intake pool was barren, weedless and fishless except for a few bullheads on the bottom. I circled it carefully and came back to the original weed-grown channel across the gridded face of the pump house. I could see the silhouetted forms of the little fish among the trailing strands of weed even from a distance. As I came closer I saw that they were coho fingerlings, unusually well grown and brilliantly colored, their caudal, pectoral and ventral fins almost scarlet instead of orange, the long outer rays of their anal fins brilliantly white, their bodies golden between the heavy parr marks. They were in successive schools of one or two hundred

as I moved slowly among them out towards the log boom,
and there were at least a thousand, perhaps twice that number, hovering over the weeds. One was a truly astonishing
fish, at least six inches long, and I could only assume that
he was holding over in fresh water for a second summer.
Yet again, they were holding in a very moderate flow and
the protection of the weed was close at hand. The three-
and four-pound cutthroats, still holding farther out by the
boom, seemed entirely unaware of their nearness, but they
would in any case have made very difficult prey.

I do not want to labor this point of the surprises that
one comes upon under water beyond saying that they are
frequent and often quite important, calling for some fairly
sharp adjustment of preconceived ideas. In time they must,
I think, lead to a markedly different overall view of any
river and its fish, still far from perfect but clearer and
more accurate than the old one.

It is hardly necessary to say that I waited for the arrival
of the salmon runs this fall with a far keener excitement
than ever before. I knew that I should be able to see a
good deal, but how much I did not know and still do not,
for there are runs still to come.

The first fish we saw were in the little school of humpbacks at the lower end of the first long pool of the canyon
on July twenty-eighth. These were not unexpected—I have
known for more than twenty years that a few humpbacks
come into that pool well before the end of July. But from
there on it has been a series of adventures and delights.

Just a week later Stan and I swam the Sandy Pool, a
magnificent stretch some four hundred yards long and
fully twenty feet deep in its deepest places. Water pours

in at the head in a powerful broken rush from the rapid above, drives under the bridge and gradually smooths out from there down, though there is a strong current along the north side through the whole length of the pool at normal flow. About a hundred and fifty yards below the bridge the pool shallows among great boulders that reach within a foot or two of the surface, then deepens again into the main holding water.

We swam the pool four times that day, crossing the broken water at the head, drifting down with the flow, crossing again at the tail and working up through the easier water near the south bank. Each time we learned a little more about the narrow eddies where we could hold on the north side, the strength of flow near the tail and the likeliest places to look for fish.

We saw very little in the upper part of the pool, but well down towards the tail, in the deepest part, there was a school of bright humpbacks that scattered each time we came over it, to re-form as soon as we had passed. And with these were some twenty or thirty great king salmon, nervous fish that swam upstream under us with enormous speed and power, easily passing the humpbacks. I was disappointed that the fish were so nervous, but it was early in the season and it seemed reasonable to expect that they would settle down later, when the dangers of salt water were farther behind them. Watching their brief flight for the third or fourth time, I noticed that at least one of the big fish seemed always headed towards a big boulder, near the mouth of the creek on the south side. The current was easy enough to let me approach the boulder from downstream, on the shoreward side. I crept up to it as softly as

I could, peered over it and saw him clearly for a fraction of time—a fine bright forty-pounder. In exactly the same moment he saw me and was gone.

From then on I swam the river pretty regularly and watched the runs build up. There had been a commercial fishing strike through most of July which probably allowed unusually large escapements. By mid-August I judged there were at least a thousand humpbacks in the Sandy Pool, spread all the way from the bridge to the tail but concentrated mainly in two or three places. The same twenty or thirty tyees still held down in the deep part of the pool and were already less nervous.

The day after this estimate I swam the Line Fence Pool, a shallow ease up between rapids that runs about a hundred yards from my upstream line fence. It is a difficult place to hold, but there was little need to hold. As I drifted down there were humpbacks everywhere I looked, clear shapes scattering from directly under me, shadowy shapes on either side and beyond them still others, dimly seen through the water and beyond these still more, seen only by the white strips of their pale bellies as the current swung them. It was a sight that made me draw deep breaths of amazement and satisfaction. I wanted to go down and touch them and welcome them, but all I could do was wish them well.

These fish, I knew, were not in the final resting place where they would ripen to spawn. Many would move on upstream and the majority would find their way into the Quinsam, a small tributary that enters on the right bank of the Campbell and offers several miles of good spawning water. Within a few days much had changed. There were still a lot of fish in the Line Fence Pool, but they were now spread out in smaller groups instead of being massed all through the pool. I was able to watch one group of four males and three females just under the foot of the rapid from a distance of four or five feet, by holding behind a sheltering boulder. They were still bright, clean fish, the males little humped as yet, but they seemed calm and settled and I thought they might well be local spawners.

In the Sandy Pool there were two or three thousand fish, most of them in an unending stream along the line of the main current, where a few big kings moved among them; but at least five hundred were packed in a solid school near the mouth of the creek. Few of these fish seemed settled. On the same day I found I could work out across the first run of the little pool just above the mouth of the Quinsam and into the quieter water between that and the heavy run that makes the main part of the pool. Looking outwards into this great rush of current, I saw the fish packed together in a long narrow mass, fish beside fish and fish above fish so closely that they were almost touching. Easing slowly along beside them, I judged the school to be two feet deep, six or eight feet wide and not less than forty feet long. There was movement in the mass, of course, but it was plain the fish were waiting and that they could only be waiting for a fresh flow of water to draw them up the Quinsam. I climbed out of the water and stood looking down at the pool. Once in two or three minutes a fish rolled somewhere, usually down towards the tail of the pool, well below the main concentration. One could have watched for an hour and guessed at no more than fifty or a hundred fish scattered under the impenetrable surface. I had to go back again to convince myself that I had really seen them—perhaps two thousand, perhaps many more.

Stan and I went several times to the long pool at the start of the canyon during August and early September. As we swam towards the head on August eleventh I saw a school of thirty or forty humpbacks down near bottom in about thirty feet of water. Watching them, I suddenly recognized a male sockeye, unmistakably green of head and red of body. Then there was another and another until I counted six in all; we dove down to see them clearly and recognized females as well. I have long known that a few, very few, sockeye run to the Campbell, because I see one or two spawning pairs among the tyees most years, but this sight suggested more than those few. Two weeks later the river was very low and we were able to swim along the lip of the surge pool; here, too, we found several male sockeye and a few females. Up near the head of the long pool, where we had seen the others, we now saw a school of at least thirty or forty. Two fine males had separated from the school and settled in full sunlight among the rocks of the bottom in only fifteen or twenty feet of water. Stan dived down and swam within two or three feet of them before they moved. "They are like jewels," he told me when he came up.

We were concerned also to be quite certain that there was no concentration of big tyees anywhere in that great pool. Visiting fishermen and their guides had been complaining that the increased flow of the Campbell draws the fish in early from salt water and that they hide out in the depths of the long pool. Some fish always do move in

during the first eight or ten days of August, and one sees
them rolling in the Island Pools and the Sandy Pool. But
the numbers are not great in proportion to the total run,
and I thought it highly unlikely that any would choose
to hide themselves in the still waters of the long pool. We
searched conscientiously through most of the pool, diving
repeatedly to bring the bottom in clear sight. There was
no sign of big fish and at last no possibility was left except
the very deep water at the start of the pool.

Here it was not so easy to find bottom, though we were
usually able to see it dimly before we turned back towards
the surface. At last Stan found the fish. I had to dive three
more times before I saw them, then I was suddenly right
on top of them, almost amongst them, as they scattered in
the semidarkness, fifteen or twenty great shadowy fish that
disappeared into deeper darkness in the very moment of
discovery.

A week or so later we dived several times again in the
same place and each time came upon about the same number of fish in much the same way. Perhaps we should have
gone down with tanks and searched more thoroughly, but
I am satisfied that no more than these few fish were there.
To find them at all was a surprise. To come upon them
as we did, so closely and suddenly in that dim gray world,
was intensely exciting, a sharing of the secret places of
the river beyond normal experience.

As fall draws on and the runs continue to come in,
experience builds on experience. It is now late September
and the fall rains have begun, freshening the streams to
draw still more fish and to move the ones already there.
On September twelfth I saw the first coho, a jack, work-

ing slowly upstream past the point of the wing dam. There
have been others since; one big fish, his neb scarred and
his tail badly torn by some deep-sea battle with troller's
hook and line, is holding at the head of the Lower Island
Pool. Alder leaves are beginning to collect in the eddies
and occasional giant broad leaves of maple, magnified to
startling proportions, drift serenely in mid-water. I have
swum the lower pools of the little Quinsam and found
them easily explored and the fish easily approached where
their room for flight is so limited. I have seen some magnificent fall cutthroats of three and perhaps four pounds and
occasional summer steelheads. But in comparison with the
hordes of salmon, both trout are pathetically few. It is hard
to understand why.

Of the six or eight pools on the Campbell below the
canyon, no two are even nearly similar, from above or
below the surface. But from below the surface their differences are emphasized and none is more beautiful than the
Lower Islands from the north bank. The old gravel bar
that used to be dry at normal water is now almost constantly covered by a foot or more of flow. The run under
the cut bank is a deep green Arthur Rackham world of
twisted tree roots, strange weeds and waterlogged drift.
One works into it from downstream, under the great sub-
merged bole of the spruce tree and slowly on up from one
exposed tree root to another. It nearly always holds one
or two good big trout and a few pre-migrant steelheads.
Near the head of the run, under the close reach of the
ground maple limbs, it is easy to slip out over the gravel
bar, now heavily grown with trailing, pale green weeds
that sway and swing in the current.

Along the edge of the steep drop-off into the fast flow of the pool, these weeds make useful shelter for a swimmer and the fish lie very close. One gray day early in September I passed that way, happily watching some four or five hundred salmon through the gaps in the weed. I passed beyond the weed and on to the bushes that reach out almost into the tear of wave-ridden current where the full force of the rapid from the Main Island breaks into the pool. I found a waterlogged cedar limb wedged between the rocks and clung to it, looking out into plunging, tossing bubbles. There were more humpbacks and then I could see the pale outline of a tyee of thirty-five or forty pounds. He was a fresh fish, and every so often the surges of current caught him and tipped his whole bright side straight up towards me in a vivid flash.

The cedar limb was firmly anchored, so I slid my grip to its extreme tip, drew myself slowly level with it and gradually extended my arm to its full length. The current lifted and twisted my body but the big fish held his station. He was very close to me now and seemed to see me, but he must have felt secure in the strong water because, if anything, he moved closer. He was about a foot above the bottom in six or eight feet of water, though the larger rocks were close under his belly. From time to time the bubbles of the breaking rapid drove right down in showers around his head and the surging current tossed him, yet he held without the slightest sign of effort. His breathing was slow and easy and once he opened his mouth wide to yawn. When the clustered humpbacks brushed against his body he paid no attention to them. He was perfect in his place, a great and powerful fish in a great and powerful river. I thought he seemed content. And why not? He was within such close reach of his life's purpose that nothing within reason could keep him from it.

Now the humpback males have shaped up their great humps and the females are beginning to dig. The big tyees are beginning to show in hundreds instead of tens and soon they will be spawning. The cohos will come in and after them the dog salmon and then, in a very short while, it will all be over. But I hope to keep looking through it all and to find the first of the winter steelheads among the last of the salmon late in November. Few fish are more secret in their movements than these and few can be more fascinating for a fisherman to watch close at hand.

5. *Underwater Learning*

THE FLY-FISHERMAN RELEASED UNDER water with mask and snorkel becomes that dangerous character, the unregenerate naturalist, free to observe without restriction and to speculate without restraint. True, the scientist is already down there, to the tip of his snorkel and far beyond. But things move a little fast for precise observation and he has not yet learned a system of exact weights and measurements; this will come in time, of course, but for a while at least the naturalist has a wholly legitimate field for his impressionistic observations and imaginative speculations, which he will undoubtedly use to generate his usual mixture of truths and old wives' tales, confusing romanticism and inspired deduction. It is a precious freedom and I like to feel that I shall serve within it with honorable and honest restraint. For there is a truth in the impressions that the eye sends to the brain as well as in the measurements that correct those impressions; and there is truth in man's emotional interpretation of the world about him, as well as in his more objective appraisals.

When the cohos first come into the river they are noble, steel-gray fish with unspotted, slightly iridescent tails. A few among them are just beginning to show a glow of spawning red. After the humpbacks they all seem very strong and large and active. They take possession of the river as though they were used to it, exploring every part, swimming freely in mid-water, pushing into the strongest currents, swimming calmly through eddies and even into still backwaters. They do not mass in schools like the humpbacks and sockeyes; they are much less nervous than the great king salmon and far more varied in their behavior. Of all the Pacific salmons the coho seems least likely to die after spawning, if only because he takes to the river so naturally and completely, and some few of them do hold on to life for a surprisingly long while; I have caught spawned-out cohos, moribund but still quite active, as late as February.

For all their calmness, the cohos seem to bring a sense of urgency to the river. Even though these early ones have come in well ahead of the fall rains, time is closing in fast. The plunging water at the foot of the rapids is grayer now, and along the edges of the river, among the sheltering boulders, golden maple leaves and scarlet dogwood leaves drift in gentle procession. A few more of the big harvest cutthroats have moved in and hold their stations with impressive regularity, day after day, three-pounders magnified to four-pounders, four-pounders to five-pounders by the water's distortion.

The sudden abundance of the cohos is no less surprising than the massive arrival of the humpback run, but it is much harder to observe. Towards the end of September I realized that I was seeing cohos all through the river, now a glimmer of gold and red among duller, white-bellied shapes of the humpbacks at the head of a pool, now a sharpness of clean silver-gray, cruising or holding in mid-water. I found them here and there through the long length of the Sandy Pool as I was searching for signs that the main body of tyees had run in. To my surprise the group of tyees that had been holding for several weeks in the deepest part of the pool seemed very little larger—perhaps fifty or sixty fish where there had been thirty or forty. I worked across the tail of the pool, as far down as I could go without becoming committed to the rapid below, and still saw only a few fish.

In the center of the tail there is a narrow slick five or six feet deep, that funnels down for some sixty or seventy yards into the rapid. I turned down into it at last and found myself sliding faster and faster over dozens of fish, tyees and cohos intermixed, scattering lazily away from my drift, showing red and gold and gray through the clear and shallow water, often so close that I could see the presence or absence of spots on their broad tail fins in spite of the speed of my passage. A moment later, my eyes still full of their grace and beauty, I was in the rapid. The great round boulders passed closely under me, the current waves bounced my body and slapped at the snorkel; once or twice I started my flippers to give me steerage way past a larger boulder, but I had time to look well about me and saw no fish. Then the roar and rush of water eased into the five-

or six-foot depth of the Line Fence Pool and I found them again, cohos in good numbers, freshly in from salt water and holding in the first resting place above tide.

A day or two after this I swam the Long Pool at the start of the canyon and found that the cohos had reached there too. Fair numbers of them were moving back and forth through the strong turbulence under the lip of the surge pool and a school of fifty or more red-sided rainbows, varying from eight to eighteen inches in length, was holding just at the edge of the turbulence. As I worked up the pool I came upon a single bright coho in the narrowest, deepest, loneliest part. He was within three or four feet of the surface, close against the pale brown algae of the rock wall, and let me come so close that I could plainly see the lazy ripples of his muscles under the shimmering skin and scales. There was another and larger fish at the head of the pool which let me approach almost as closely before he turned back under me towards deeper water.

On the way back down the pool, again in what I think of as the lonely part, where the towering walls are steepest and tallest and the bottom is lost beyond sight, I noticed that the water was suddenly bright about me. It was bright with the bodies of the rainbow school, moving lazily upstream. They seemed to pause and turn to examine me, even as I paused and turned to examine them. Two of the fish had scars on their sides that established them as the same group I had seen near the lip of the surge pool. One bright healthy little fish, ten or twelve inches long, close to the average of the school, had a broken lower jaw, hanging vertically downwards from the line of his head. Yet he swam as calmly and effectively as any of the others.

I watched him closely and the distorted set of the jaw was rigid and unchanging. It seems difficult to imagine an injury that would produce such an effect, and I have wondered since if it could be a deformity that had been with him from the egg. If so, it seems a minor miracle that he has been able to survive and grow in the face of what must be an immense handicap in feeding, swimming and even breathing.

A few days later, early in October, I swam the Lower Island Pool in search of the tyees that I knew must be resting there. Twice I drifted carefully down in the easy flow along the edge of the heavy current, but all I found were a few humpbacks and two or three cohos. I worked up along the edge of the pool again and as far out as I could under the break of the rapid, then swam two or three strokes to get into the main rush of the current. It was a swift passage. In the main body of the pool, under the white current waves, I saw a few cohos. Then I was over the tyees, great, powerful, bronze fish of thirty and forty and fifty pounds, scattering in every direction from my drift. I was still among them when I swung over to avoid being carried down into the next rapid, but I knew I had seen eighty or a hundred in the few short seconds of drifting over them; the total number in the pool must have been several times that, all concentrated near bottom in the line of the heaviest flow.

As I came out of the water I found myself trying to imagine a pool filled with five or six hundred Atlantic salmon of thirty pounds and upward and the sort of sport one could expect from it. It struck me then that Atlantic salmon would not be lying as these fish were, closely grouped near bottom in that formidable rush of current. Instead they would have been scattered through the pool, generally in softer and much more fishable holding water. From that thought it was an easy step to the idea that the holding and resting habits of migratory fish may play a much more important part in determining whether or not they are likely to take than any simple inclination or disinclination to strike.

No fisherman would really expect to move a heavy fish up to a fly through such water, nor could he have any serious hope of being able to work the fly down near bottom. He might expect to do better with lure or bait, and he would be right; but in proportion to the numbers of fish available his results would still be unimpressive. Only when the big fish approach maturity and move out to easier, shallower water is there likely to be any great change in their responsiveness.

Cohos do respond a good deal more readily to fly or lure or bait, though still not well in proportion to their numbers. The explanation of this may be in their much greater mobility and restlessness. At any given time they may be found in good numbers lying in much the same type of water as the tyees, but there are always a certain number of wanderers who may be found almost anywhere and it seems likely that these are the ones that respond to the fisherman. It seems likely, too, that the coho's relatively calm and familiar acceptance of the river may reflect his full year of river life before migration and the short span of his ocean life.

It is interesting to compare the numbers and availability of steelhead in the same river. Through August, September and October, I have seen thousands of humpbacks, hundreds of tyees and cohos and somewhere between fifty and a hundred sockeyes. In the same length of time I have not seen more than twenty summer steelhead, yet in any season when I fish the river at all regularly during these months I catch at least half a dozen, often considerably more, all on the fly. It is only possible to conclude that steelhead, under normal water conditions, are extremely responsive fish.

Migratory cutthroat trout are more difficult to assess. Before the river was dammed and the canyon flow turned through the powerhouse, August was the ideal fishing month for really big cutthroats in fair abundance, with September almost equally good, though by then the fish were falling off slightly in condition. Though I searched the river thoroughly below the surface during August I saw very few cutthroats and none that I judged to be over two pounds. In September they began to appear, scattered here and there and often in places that a fisherman would normally pass by. There was no precise pattern, but they tended to be near the edge of fast, deep water that offered protection, in stations that made for calm and easy resting yet offered fairly good possibilities of drifting feed. Generally they were well down in the water, seemingly content and inactive. They were far less nervous than either salmon or steelhead, though they were watchful and would not permit a clumsy or too familiar approach. A few smaller fish, of two pounds or less, were in more active feeding stations, usually close under the banks, but again in places that one might easily pass without fishing.

There are obvious difficulties in this type of behavior,

the most obvious being the rather unlikely choice of station and the lazy, almost lethargic mood of the big fish. Most of them, I thought, would have responded to the slow swing of a silver-bodied wet fly very near them or to repeated and accurate drifts of a large floating fly. But it would be easy to disturb them with a downstream approach unless one knew exactly where they were, while the dry-fly fisherman, working up from below, would almost certainly pass over them too quickly.

A few of the big fish were in more active feeding stations —the places where one usually finds them and catches them. But they were not holding at all steadily, and I am convinced that this is another difficulty that must often defeat the angler. One day I made a very successful approach on a really good fish in the run under the cut bank on the north side of the Lower Island Pool. When I first saw the fish he was fifteen or twenty feet upstream from me, within six inches of the bank, just behind a protruding upright branch on which several dead maple leaves were caught. He was well up in the water and obviously willing to feed, but his tight position was still further protected by a long overhang of ground maple branches. A wet fly on a long line, drifted from upstream closely past the protruding limb, would almost certainly have risen him; but the risk of hooking into the limb or the leaves would have been considerable, and while he might have moved out to a less accurate cast, the rise would probably have been short.

Though it would have been a difficult cast, a dry fly from below, placed closely against the limb, would certainly have risen and hooked the fish. But it is not the sort of cast one would normally risk or consider necessary.

Most of us, I think, would have felt the run well covered by a cast considerably farther out from the bank, especially as the fish was so very close to the head of the run.

These thoughts ran through my mind as I watched the big fish through the blue-green water and I promised myself to mark the spot well and remember it. The fish seemed quite unaware of me still and I was well placed in the run, four or five feet out from the cut bank and with a firm hold on a tangle of waterlogged brush, so I decided to watch for a while longer. I saw him move slightly to intercept something drifting in the water then, quite suddenly, he was in a new position, about three feet out from the bank and almost in the center of the run. At first I thought he was holding, then I saw he was drifting very gradually back and in towards the bank again. When he was within a foot or so of the bank he turned out again and slowly swung across the run, still drifting almost imperceptibly downstream. About ten minutes later he had worked down to a position in the center of the run, no more than three feet from where my left hand clung to the brush. I could see every spot on his heavy golden body, every ripple and change of set in his fins, even the sheen of red just developing on his gill covers. While I watched he raised himself some six inches through the water, opened his mouth widely and took in a small gray piece of drift, no more than half an inch long. I could not tell what it was, but he bit once on it with a fierce grip of his wide jaws and swallowed it.

From that point he began to work upstream again just as slowly as he had worked down. There was no sign at all that he had seen me, yet there is not much doubt he was

aware of me as an unusual shape among the familiar shapes
of the run; if I had not been there, his downstream drift
would certainly have continued. I moved slightly to change
my grip on the brush pile, but there was no sign of change
in his own deliberate movement. When he was six or eight
feet upstream I slowly changed position and lifted my head
above water to clear my snorkel. When I looked back, he
was gone.

Apart from the sheer pleasure of watching a fine fish in
his calm pursuits at such close range, this brief observation
suggested to me that it must often be unsound to assume
that certain places—those where we have risen fish—are the
precise spots where we should expect to find fish again.
The run, as I have said, is quite fast, the sort of place where
one would expect a good fish to hold and wait for food.
Yet this particular fish had ranged nearly fifteen feet downstream and some four or five feet back and forth across
the stream while I watched, and I am satisfied that he would
have taken a properly presented fly at any point in this
movement. The lesson seems to be that a run of this sort
must be fished with care and precision from top to bottom
and across its full width, even when one thinks one knows
the best holding places.

My friends have been quick to point out that the ethics
of spying on fish under water in this way are highly ques-
tionable. I suppose they are. But I find I have practically
no desire to go out and try to catch the fish I have seen
while diving; I would rather go back and have another
look at them. By the time I have watched the same fish
twice, he is an old friend and I wouldn't dream of going
out to kill him; I would even hesitate to disturb him by

catching him and putting him back. The more general observations about where fish lie and how they behave will certainly influence my future fishing methods to some extent, but I don't expect from them any miracles of achievement that will trouble my conscience.

A much more serious question, at once ethical and practical, does concern me. It is the degree of disturbance caused to maturing salmon by the passing of a diver in a river. I feel I have learned a good deal about how to find the fish and how to approach them and I use all the skill I can find to avoid disturbing them—after all, the point is to watch them, count them, study them, not to chase them. But even so, it is obvious to me that I often do disturb them, especially the big king salmon, to the point of brief panic. Even when they are ten or twenty feet under me they drive away with a tremendous burst of power that carries them out of sight in a moment of time.

Once a Pacific salmon leaves salt water, the reserve of energy left to him to complete his journey and his spawning is closely limited. By measurement he has been shown to use about seventy-five per cent of his available energy in his normal activities. Any significant degree of stress beyond this point may impair his spawning or even cause death before spawning.

The question then seems to be: what is a significant degree of stress? Both humpbacks and cohos will start swiftly away from a clumsy approach or from a downstream approach, but they do not drive nearly so hard and fast as the kings and they slow up and settle down almost immediately, often while still in sight. I feel satisfied that the strain of this evasion is not very great, even when they are freshly in from salt water and far more nervous than they later become.

In spite of its initial speed, the drive that takes a king salmon well beyond sight of a swimmer need not be more than twenty or thirty yards, and I do not think the fish normally go farther than this. When I circle back along the edge of the pool to look for them again I nearly always find them back where they were before. A fast flight of this length is less than a quarter of the drive a hooked king salmon puts into his first long run. In my experience one can allow for another hour of vigorous performance after this run before a fish of thirty or forty pounds can be brought to hand on a fly rod, and even then he will rapidly recover enough energy to swim away with power when the fly is released. It seems safe to conclude from this that a swimmer passing over the fish once, twice or even three times in fairly quick succession will probably do them little or no harm.

When I am watching the salmon I usually swim alone or, more rarely, with a single companion. So far I have yet to meet another diver on the river. Whenever possible I avoid swimming directly downstream over large groups of resting fish, and it is necessary to do so only when attempting to make an estimate of the timing and numbers of a new run. The real pleasure of watching the fish is far better served by the cunning and careful approaches one can make along the edges of the pools, by circling with the eddies or along the line of shelter behind large boulders. But I sometimes wonder what the effect might be if, as may well happen, divers chose to take to the rivers in considerable numbers. Would the fish quickly become used to the passing figures or would they continue to waste their energy in violent flight?

It is only the fish that are newly returned from distant ocean traveling that are so easily disturbed. Trout, even migratory cutthroats, are far less nervous and seem to become readily used to the close approach of a swimmer. Though I have not swum over them, I suspect that Atlantic salmon would be little, if at all, more nervous and flighty than are the cohos and it seems logical to believe, too, that expenditure of energy would be far less critical for them than for Pacific salmon. But I think it is well for all of us who go into the rivers to watch fish under water to remember that we are intruders. The least we can do is treat the fish and their domain with respect and train ourselves to subtle ways of observation instead of exposing ourselves as objects of terror.

6. *At Winter's Edge*

I T IS NEARLY THE END OF OCTOBER NOW
and the heavy rains have come at last, with gales of wind
from the southeast. Creeks that were dry or almost dry
two weeks ago are foaming seaward with muddy brown
waters. It is time and more than time for the dog salmon
to come and complete the year's return. Have they come
in? Are they going to come? I don't really know.

Four or five days ago I went out to look for them in
the Line Fence Pool, where they should show first. It was
a foolish choice because the Quinsam was high and muddy
from the weekend rains and I could see scarcely anything
at all. Just as I pushed out into the fast water I caught a
shadowy glimpse of a fish that seemed to have a dog
salmon's shape and markings. I thought I should see others
on my way down the pool, but the only fish I saw were a
few cohos.

A day or two later I saw half a dozen dog salmon in

Cook Creek, which had been almost dry a week earlier but now was running low and clear. Last night I talked with two purse-seine skippers who were starting south to store their salmon nets and go out for winter herring. "No fish coming through," they said. "Nothing to stay out there for."

"Maybe they're late," I suggested.

"No," said one. "It must be the Japs are getting them all."

It is unlikely. Comparatively few North American dog salmon, even from Alaska, go more than ten degrees beyond the abstention line at 175° W Longitude, and there is nothing to suggest that Canadian fish reach the line. Yet the decline in the runs has been dramatic and obvious. The five-year average commercial catch from 1950 to 1954 was fifty-eight million pounds; from 1955 to 1959 it was twenty-seven million pounds; in the three years from 1960 to 1962 the average had dropped to seventeen million pounds. Thirty years ago I remember dog salmon running to the Nimpkish River in such numbers that one commonly saw thirty or forty fish in the air at once. Every rapid and shallow was full of them and the bottoms of the slower reaches were hidden by swaying masses of fish. At night they splashed along the edges of the river in manifold, unceasing sound. Then, and for many seasons after, they were the purse-seine fishermen's late-fall standby; however badly the rest of the season had gone, however low the price, he could depend on saving something out of it all on the dog salmon. Now, though the price has increased tenfold, it is no longer worth his while to stay out in the autumn gales to look for them.

Does this have any meaning for an angler? I think it has. It is true that the dog salmon has never been considered a game fish; he runs so late in the year and so straight to the rivers from the ocean that there is little opportunity to fish for him. But his rapid and unexplained decline is a reminder of the sensitivity of the runs and their still mysterious nature. I do not think we shall lose the dog salmon runs; I think rather that we shall be able to build them back to their former abundance. But until we know and understand the reasons for the decline and develop measures to counteract it I do not think we can feel easy about any of the runs.

The salmon have survived the natural catastrophes of the rivers and the ocean through many thousands of years, which is reason enough to suppose that they will be able to survive them for many thousands of years to come. Twenty years ago it was inconceivable that any act of man could seriously modify the nature of the North Pacific Ocean. Today the possibility is still remote, but by no means inconceivable. The machinery of nuclear pollution is well within reach; a grandiose scheme for damming the Bering Strait and exchanging arctic for Pacific water has been discussed—how seriously, I do not know. But engineers can do anything if the money is found for it, and all too often it is found.

If these threats are still remote, a third one is not. The past twenty years have seen a spectacular increase in the sophistication and efficiency of the world's high-seas fishing fleets. There are new and better ways of finding fish, of catching them, of processing them and preserving them. No distance is too great, no weather is too formidable, no technical problem remains insoluble. The world's demand for the yield of the seas steadily increases and will inevitably go on increasing. Few of the old protections that allowed individual nations to control and manage their offshore fisheries can still have effect. The old three-mile limit of territorial waters has long been meaningless and some nations have recognized this by extending the limit. But for wide-ranging fish like the salmon no enforceable limit can possibly provide adequate protection. The only possible answer is in international co-operation that recognizes the origin of the fish and respects the rights of the nations that protect their breeding and rearing, because if these rights are not respected there will be no good reason to continue protection and the runs will inevitably be allowed to die.

The breeding and rearing areas of the salmon are the streams and rivers and lakes. The salmon runs are fitted and adapted to them with an exactitude that permits little change. Yet the changes of civilization are relentless and unceasing, sometimes subtle, sometimes overt, almost invariably detrimental. It is impossible to overstate the biological precision of the salmon, almost equally impossible to find an engineer, a forester, a miner, a city planner, a politician or an industrialist who can understand it. Pollution of a stream, for instance, whether through industrial wastes, sewage, crop spraying or forest spraying, need not kill fish to destroy salmon runs. It need only force them, through high temperatures or low oxygen values, to an overexpenditure of energy in their upstream passage. The result will be spawning failure or even death before spawning.

Even on a great river system like that of the Fraser, controlled and managed by international agreement, closely studied from year to year, catastrophes that emphasize the narrow tolerance of the runs occur with depressing regularity. The record Adams River run of 1958, which yielded more than eighteen million fish in the catch and a spawning escapement of two million, produced only enough spawners to seed the beds in 1962. Why? There were enough downstream migrants in the spring of 1960 to promise a catch of ten or twelve million fish in 1962. They reached the estuary at a time of unusually low river flow and unfavorable temperatures. The informed presumption is that they were unable to withstand the stress of adjustment to salt water.

In 1961 a great escapement of sockeyes got through to the Horsefly River. The fish were early, water temperatures were high and made higher by a bad forest fire. Most of the fish died without spawning. In 1963, the year in which I write, eight hundred thousand sockeyes ran through to the Chilco River. The fish were ten days early. They were in excessive numbers because a commercial strike had let too many through. Again the early season temperatures were high. Of the eight hundred thousand, only eighty thousand survived to spawn. Exactly why the others died is not yet known, but in a sense it scarcely matters. They died of excessive stress in one form or another, a strain on energy reserves that was beyond their tolerance.

A run can, of course, build back from a disaster of this sort in two or three successful cycles; it seems likely that similar disasters, through mistiming and unfavorable weather conditions, may have occurred long before there was any significant interference by mankind. But there is pollution now in the lower reaches of the Fraser. Under normal conditions the fish pass through it successfully. But when other conditions approach the limits of tolerance this additional stress must have its effect. Without its extra demand on them, perhaps the Adams River smolts would have survived in 1960, perhaps this year's Chilco run would have spawned successfully.

Dams, irrigation and headwater logging are all factors that can and do affect the runs, sometimes immediately and disastrously, more often by subtle and cumulative attritions. And any combinations of these factors with each other or with the stresses of pollution, even though none may be lethal in itself, can lead to disaster or total destruction.

To industrial man a river is just a lot of water running down a natural channel in the earth in rather untidy fashion. He is quick to assume that he can handle it all much better. Up to a point he is likely to be right, but he has not so far shown himself very adept at discerning just where the point of error begins; often he does not seem to care so long as his own small purpose is achieved. Rivers and the watersheds that make them are infinitely complicated and demand a great deal more understanding and respect than most developers bother to give them.

These things make the problems of today, which are frightening enough. The problems of tomorrow go far beyond them. North Americans are already using water several times over, in some instances drinking each other's detergents. This is only a beginning of scarcity. I have heard it said that within fifty years no river in the United States will reach the ocean; the water will all be used before it gets that far. Something of the sort is by no means impossible. It will not happen suddenly or dramatically, but little by little, almost imperceptibly. And long before that time heavy and intense demand will have come upon those parts of the continent that have water "to spare." The salmon country—the Pacific Northwest, British Columbia and Alaska—has water, conceivably even some to spare. The prairie provinces of Canada have already claimed some color of right in the headwaters of the Columbia and the Fraser, pointing out that they can be turned back over and through the Rockies; California, improvident, ambitious and insatiable, no doubt has roughly similar thoughts. The ultimate fate of the salmon runs may depend on the definition of the phrase "water to spare" unless economic means of converting vast quantities of salt water into fresh are soon found. It seems a project that would have a good deal more immediate purpose and meaning than landing a man on the moon, for North America and the rest of the world. In comparison with the moon project its cost need scarcely disturb the most reluctant taxpayer.

I am afraid for the future, as I suppose every thinking person must be. Yet even on this dark and sodden late October day I can feel hope and find assurance that something will be left long years from now of all I have seen and known. Yesterday, under the racing clouds and the drive of the rain, I went out again to look for the dog salmon. The Quinsam was muddy and strong all along the right bank of the Campbell, and the Campbell itself was rising, so it was useless to look in the Line Fence Pool or the Sandy Pool. Because the day was so formidable with its darkness and rain and gusty wind, and because I was alone, I promised myself I would look only briefly and chose the small pool just above the mouth of the Quinsam.

I went in part way up the rapid immediately above the pool. Rain drops spurted little jets all over the surface of the water, but the roar and race of the storm was lost at once in the rush and hiss of the rapid. The moment my face mask was under the surface film I felt only the turbulent peace of the murky green water. Ahead of me the whitened body of a king salmon hung upside down behind a big boulder; I worked up to it, saw the narrow back and flattened belly and knew that the fish had spawned, then pushed out into the tearing current and went down with it, working out and across. Two enormous kings, one red, one black, fled from me and I recognized a few cohos with them and below them. The tail of the pool came up fast and I had to cut in, then drive with my flippers to reach the eddy.

The floor of the eddy is deep and broken, with big boulders resting under shelves and overhangs of hard, pale clay. Leaves from every kind of tree swung and twisted in it, green and brown and gold, red and buff and black, over the buff and green of the sponge-grown boulders below. Under the leaves yet with them, the white wraiths of half a dozen spawned-out humpbacks ceaselessly swirled in weightless death, pale shapes teased into motions of life by the currents that played among the boulders.

I swam the pool several times again but still saw no dog salmon, though I have little doubt that at least a few were there. Coming into the eddy for the last time I noticed a branch caught among the boulders and a frayed rope hanging from it. Something glinted briefly as the rope swayed in the flow at the edge of the eddy. I dove down and came up with two tiny spinners left by some summer fisherman.

Today the storm has passed and the gulls are screaming

over the racing river, diving to pick up waste eggs and other drift that comes down after the spawning. The humpbacks are finished now, but within a few days the river will be down again. In the Island Pools I shall find the big kings spawning where six solid feet of flow is rushing by today. There will be cohos among them and a few humpbacks miraculously holding on to life. I shall find the dog salmon at last, whether many or few, and I shall wonder again what it is they need to build back to the multitudes of thirty years ago. For the time being the runs are in and the Campbell protects her own. Next month I shall look for the main body of the cutthroat run, from above the surface with a fly rod, from below the surface with face mask and snorkel. Only a little after them will come the splendid gray shapes of the first winter steelhead.

7. *Ethics Again*

WHEN A FISHERMAN TAKES TO THE FACE
mask and snorkel, his purpose must inevitably be suspect;
he is hoping to learn how to catch more fish. It would be
hard to prove otherwise, unless one abandoned rod and
line altogether, which I do not propose to do. It would be
impossible not to benefit in some degree from experience
under water. The ethical question, if there is one, is: how
directly? And perhaps also: how much?

I have said that I will carry neither death nor fear with
me under water if I can help it. I have no wish to disturb
the peace that exists between underwater man and underwater animals. I would far rather build it and strengthen it
if I can. Wild animal life unafraid of man and largely unaware of him is to me a thing most precious and desirable.
So far as I know, game fish everywhere are protected by
law from underwater attack or disturbance and certainly
trout and salmon in fresh water are protected; my own

intention goes well beyond this. I do not wish to injure or threaten anything that swims when I am under water.

I am not concerned to go beyond this and extend my peace agreement to cover man above the surface film of the water because I believe the two are quite separate. The ordinary attacks of man above the water are not identifiable with man under water and so cannot create fear of him. And the fisherman above the water is at such disadvantage in his efforts to affect the fish that his sport seems legitimate.

Is it then justifiable to go under water in the guise of a friend, come out and put to use from above the water whatever knowledge has been gained by this espionage? It is, I admit, a tender question. I can answer only emotionally, not logically. I feel no desire whatsoever to go out to catch and kill a fish I have shortly before been observing sympathetically and peacefuly. I am at times tempted to go out and catch such a fish, mark him for future identification and return him to the water and I hope to do this from time to time; but I have not done it yet.

Another test I apply to the ethics of my actions is *purpose*. What am I doing down there? What am I trying to find out? Answers to these questions are easy. I am doing little beyond looking and enjoying. I want to learn more about rivers and fish, but not necessarily for the purpose of catching fish. I am curious, inquisitive, impressionable and probably romantic, but I am not deadly, nor in any way malevolent. I even hope that what I learn may do the fish some good. But I admit that this purpose is secondary to the simple pleasures of seeing the fish and the river bed and feeling the water about me.

Finally, there is a pragmatic test. How effectively can

knowledge gathered under water be applied to catching fish with a fly? There can be no doubt that it gives a better idea of where and when to look for fish. It may or may not give some useful ideas about how fish feed and what they feed on. But when this is said the fisherman still is not very much farther ahead. He still has to do the right thing in the right way to catch his fish.

So far I have had little opportunity or inclination to test the information I gain under water by fishing. But a few days ago, when I swam the pulp-mill intake pool, I found myself urgently desiring two or three of the scarlet-tailed coho fingerlings for my aquarium. I was also more than a little curious about the big cutthroats lying by the concrete blocks just inside the log boom; how big were they, could they be moved up to a fly in that rather awkward place and if they would come for it, could they be landed among the perils of the concrete blocks, hanging cables and boom chains and the boom itself? Later on the same afternoon I had seen two good fish, one of them very good, in the run under the cut bank in the Lower Island Pool. I knew they could be taken, but I wondered how long they would stay there.

With all these thoughts in mind it was natural to call my friend Van Egan the following Saturday. Van is an excellent fly-fisherman. He also teaches biology at the high school where he has a small aquarium, and only a week or so earlier he had asked me about getting a few young salmon for it. Van was interested, so we started out together on a soaking wet Saturday afternoon. I appointed myself to the task of catching six coho fingerlings and gave Van the job of working on the cutthroats. I thought he would probably

rise one to a floating fly but, from the depth at which the
fish were lying, I felt his chances of hooking it would be
no better than fifty-fifty. If he hooked it I gave him a one-
in-three chance of bringing it safely out from among the
assorted hazards. My own task, I felt sure, was quite simple.
I started out with a No. 18 fly on a 5x leader and the
little fish jumped all over it. At the end of five minutes or
more I hadn't hooked a single one. So I changed to a fly
on a No. 14 hook and did a little better. The first cast
hooked a fish, which I safely released in the bucket, but I
missed the next twenty rises in succession.

Van, meanwhile, was floating a big hair-winged fly nicely
over where the cutthroats should have been. It was a miserable place to reach and the current gave the fly little help.
I thought of those enormous golden-yellow fish looking up
from their stations near bottom without a flicker of interest
or, worse still, staring morosely dead ahead in the hope
that some unwary bullhead would stir within reach. Then
I remembered there had been two or three smaller fish
among the big ones and felt more hopeful.

I turned back to the fingerlings. My rod was much too
stiff for the quickness of strike I needed, but I did a little
better by letting the fly drag on a tight line downstream
and eventually had six handsome fingerlings in the bucket.

By this time Van had hooked a six-inch yearling steelhead and had changed to a wet fly. The wet fly was a good
deal harder to work effectively and did no better than the
dry. I began to wonder whether the fish were there at all
and showed him where I had seen a very good fish, probably a summer steelhead, lying outside the boom, in the
main river. He went off to try for it while I tried for the

fish inside the boom. They were no more interested in my
flies than his, and he had misunderstood my directions
about the fish outside the boom and fished over it, so we
decided to go on up to the Lower Island Pool. "At least I
know they'll take there," I said. "You'll probably get both
of them."

I was almost right. Van twice saw a flash from the big
fish at the downstream end of the run, but could not rise
him. He rose and hooked the other fish, a fine little summer
steelhead of about two pounds.

When I assess all this in terms of what I had learned
under water only two days previously, I am not impressed.
True, if I hadn't been out we might not have gone fishing
at all. If I hadn't seen how brigthly colored the little cohos
over the weed in the intake were, I might not have coveted
them and the aquarium fish would have come from somewhere else. If I hadn't seen the big cutthroats inside the
boom we wouldn't have bothered to throw a fly over them.
But it didn't do us any good and if I hadn't been bothering
with those fish I should certainly have directed Van more
closely to the fish outside the boom, because I always fish
there anyway; and he might very well have caught it. Thus
far, then, underwater knowledge had affected the freedom
of six fingerlings, at least one of which has already been
safely returned to the river, and had possibly saved the life
of one four-pound summer steelhead. As for the two fish
in the cut-bank run of the Lower Island, their peace would
would have been disturbed anyway, because I never pass
near the pool without drifting a fly over that particular run.

As Van said, though, it is nice to be fishing for fish when
you know they are there. Perhaps he should have said:

when you know they have been there. This, I suspect, may well be the greatest short-term advantage of underwater knowledge. It can add a good deal to the keenness and interest with which one fishes over a pool or a run and it may very well reveal good fish lying in places hitherto untested. But there is also an excellent chance that these untested places will be places where the fish do not respond well, otherwise they would be known already. Just recently, for instance, I saw two good cutthroats lying about a hundred feet below the bridge in the Sandy Pool. They were over sandy bottom, in what is almost an eddy, about ten feet from the bank and facing in towards it. What they were doing there, I do not know, but no rational fisherman would think of throwing a fly in that direction and I doubt very much that the fish could be persuaded to take if he did. Not that I shan't give it a try next time I am up that way.

Even from under the surface film, even from behind the clear-seeing, but not clairvoyant, face mask, knowledge builds only haltingly, slowly and imperfectly. Diving is not a substitute for going fishing, though it can in its own right be just as absorbingly interesting. It is simply a natural supplement, irresistible to anyone who is as curious about the ways of fish as I am, full of joy for anyone who craves new experience, full of richest satisfaction for anyone who loves the beauty of moving water, its shaped and tumbled rocks, its trailing weeds and the bright bubbles of its turbulence.

After all these years and all these many writings, perhaps I should say I have written my last of fish and fishing. But I feel it is quite unlikely that I have. Fish are still mysterious creatures and the waters of the world, deep or shallow, quiet or flowing, are still mysterious places. Both remain fascinating. I have many questions still to answer about the way of a fish with a fly and many more still about the ways of fish in their own affairs. I hope to swim and dive, as well as fish, in many new rivers, through all the seasons. If I write henceforth in two dimensions, of what I see below the surface film as well as what I see and learn from above it, I trust this will not make me less a fisherman. For I love and respect the sport no less than I always have.